The Lives of the Twelve Caesars

Nero Claudius Caesar.

The Lives of the Twelve Caesars

Nero Claudius Caesar.
by G. Suetonius Tranquillus

©2011 SMK Books

This book is a product of its time and does not reflect the same values as it would if it were written today. Parents might wish to discuss with their children how views on race have changed before allowing them to read this classic work.

All rights reserved. Printed in the United States of America. No part of this book may be used or reproduced in any manner without written permission except for brief quotations for review purposes only.

Wilder Publications, LLC.
PO Box 3005
Radford VA 24143-3005

ISBN 10: 1-61720-534-6
ISBN 13: 978-1-61720-534-7

Nero Claudius Caesar.

I. Two celebrated families, the Calvini and Aenobarbi, sprung from the race of the Domitii. The Aenobarbi derive both their extraction and their cognomen from one Lucius Domitius, of whom we have this tradition: —As he was returning out of the country to Rome, he was met by two young men of a most august appearance, who desired him to announce to the senate and people a victory, of which no certain intelligence had yet reached the city. To prove that they were more than mortals, they stroked his cheeks, and thus changed his hair, which was black, to a bright colour, resembling that of brass; which mark of distinction descended to his posterity, for they had generally red beards. This family had the honour of seven consulships , one triumph , and two censorships ; and being admitted into the patrician order, they continued the use of the same cognomen, with no other praenomina than those of Cneius and Lucius. These, however, they assumed with singular irregularity; three persons in succession sometimes adhering to one of them, and then they were changed alternately. For the first, second, and third of the Aenobarbi had the praenomen of Lucius, and again the three following, successively, that of Cneius, while those who came after were called, by turns, one, Lucius, and the other, Cneius. It appears to me proper to give a short account of several of the family, to show that Nero so far degenerated from the noble qualities of his ancestors, that he retained only their vices; as if those alone had been transmitted to him by his descent.

II. To begin, therefore, at a remote period, his great-grandfather's grandfather, Cneius Domitius, when he was tribune of the people, being offended with the high priests for electing another than himself in the room of his father, obtained the transfer of the right of election from the colleges of the priests to the people. In his consulship , having conquered the Allobroges and the Arverni , he made a progress through the province, mounted upon an elephant, with a body of soldiers attending him, in a sort of triumphal pomp. Of this person the orator Licinius Crassus said, "It was no wonder he had a brazen beard, who had a face of iron, and a heart of lead." His son, during his praetorship , proposed that Cneius Caesar, upon the expiration of his consulship, should be called to account before the senate for his administration of that office, which was supposed to be contrary both to the omens and the laws. Afterwards, when he was consul himself , he tried to deprive Cneius of the command of the army, and having been, by intrigue and cabal, appointed his successor, he was made prisoner at Corsinium, in the beginning of the civil war. Being set at liberty, he went to Marseilles, which was then besieged; where having, by his presence, animated the people to hold out, he suddenly deserted them, and at last was slain in the battle of Pharsalia. He was a man of little constancy, and of a sullen temper. In despair of his fortunes, he had recourse to poison, but was so terrified at the thoughts of death, that, immediately repenting, he took a vomit to throw it up again, and gave freedom to his physician for having, with great prudence and wisdom, given him only a gentle dose of the poison. When Cneius Pompey was consulting with his friends in what manner he should conduct himself towards those who were neuter and took no part in the contest, he was the only one who proposed that they should be treated as enemies.

III. He left a son, who was, without doubt, the best of the family. By the Pedian law, he was condemned, although innocent, amongst others who were concerned in the death of Caesar . Upon this, he went over to Brutus and Cassius, his near relations; and, after their death, not only kept together the fleet, the command of which had been given him some time before, but even increased it. At last, when the party had everywhere been defeated, he voluntarily surrendered it to Mark Antony; considering it as a piece of service for which the latter owed him no small obligations. Of all those who were condemned by the law above-mentioned, he was the only man who was restored to his country, and filled the highest offices. When the civil war again broke out, he was appointed lieutenant under the same Antony, and offered the chief command by those who were ashamed of Cleopatra; but not daring, on account of a sudden indisposition with which he was seized, either to accept or refuse it, he went over to Augustus , and died a few days after, not without an aspersion cast upon his memory. For Antony gave out, that he was induced to change sides by his impatience to be with his mistress, Servilia Nais.

IV. This Cneius had a son, named Domitius, who was afterwards well known as the nominal purchaser of the family property left by Augustus's will ; and no less famous in his youth for his dexterity in chariot-driving, than he was afterwards for the triumphal ornaments which he obtained in the German war. But he was a man of great arrogance, prodigality, and cruelty. When he was aedile, he obliged Lucius Plancus, the censor, to give him the way; and in his praetorship, and consulship, he made Roman knights and married women act on the stage. He gave hunts of wild beasts, both in the Circus and in all the wards of the city; as also a show of gladiators; but with such barbarity, that Augustus, after privately reprimanding him, to no purpose, was obliged to restrain him by a public edict.

V. By the elder Antonia he had Nero's father, a man of execrable character in every part of his life. During his attendance upon Caius Caesar in the East, he killed a freedman of his own, for refusing to drink as much as he ordered him. Being dismissed for this from Caesar's society, he did not mend his habits; for, in a village upon the Appian road, he suddenly whipped his horses, and drove his chariot, on purpose, over a poor boy, crushing him to pieces. At Rome, he struck out the eye of a Roman knight in the Forum, only for some free language in a dispute between them. He was likewise so fraudulent, that he not only cheated some silversmiths of the price of goods he had bought of them, but, during his praetorship, defrauded the owners of chariots in the Circensian games of the prizes due to them for their victory. His sister, jeering him for the complaints made by the leaders of the several parties, he agreed to sanction a law, "That, for the future, the prizes should be immediately paid." A little before the death of Tiberius, he was prosecuted for treason, adulteries, and incest with his sister Lepida, but escaped in the timely change of affairs, and died of a dropsy, at Pyrgi; leaving behind him his son, Nero, whom he had by Agrippina, the daughter of Germanicus.

VI. Nero was born at Antium, nine months after the death of Tiberius, upon the eighteenth of the calends of January [15th December], just as the sun rose, so that its beams touched him before they could well reach the earth. While many fearful conjectures, in respect to his future fortune, were formed by different persons, from the circumstances of his nativity, a saying of his father, Domitius, was regarded as an ill presage, who told his friends who were congratulating him upon the occasion, "That nothing but what was detestable, and pernicious to the public, could ever be produced of him and Agrippina." Another manifest prognostic of his future infelicity occurred upon his lustration day. For Caius Caesar being requested by his sister to give the child what name he thought proper—looking at his uncle, Claudius, who afterwards, when emperor, adopted Nero, he gave his: and this not seriously, but only in jest; Agrippina treating it with contempt, because Claudius at that time was a mere laughing-stock at the palace. He lost his father when he was three years old, being left heir to a third part of his estate; of which he never got possession, the whole being seized by his co-heir, Caius. His mother being soon after banished, he lived with his aunt Lepida, in a very necessitous condition, under the care of two tutors, a dancing-master and a barber. After Claudius came to the empire, he not only recovered his father's estate, but was enriched with the additional inheritance of that of his step-father, Crispus Passienus. Upon his mother's recall from banishment, he was advanced to such favour, through Nero's powerful interest with the emperor, that it was reported, assassins were employed by Messalina, Claudius's wife, to strangle him, as Britannicus's rival, whilst he was taking his noon-day repose. In addition to the story, it was said that they were frightened by a serpent, which crept from under his cushion, and ran away. The tale was occasioned by finding on his couch, near the pillow, the skin of a snake, which, by his mother's order, he wore for some time upon his right arm, inclosed in a bracelet of gold. This amulet, at last, he laid aside, from aversion to her memory; but he sought for it again, in vain, in the time of his extremity.

VII. When he was yet a mere boy, before he arrived at the age of puberty, during the celebration of the Circensian games, he performed his part in the Trojan play with a degree of firmness which gained him great applause. In the eleventh year of his age, he was adopted by Claudius, and placed under the tuition of Annaeus Seneca, who had been made a senator. It is said, that Seneca dreamt the night after, that he was giving a lesson to Caius Caesar. Nero soon verified his dream, betraying the cruelty of his disposition in every way he could. For he attempted to persuade his father that his brother, Britannicus, was nothing but a changeling, because the latter had saluted him, notwithstanding his adoption, by the name of Aenobarbus, as usual. When his aunt, Lepida, was brought to trial, he appeared in court as a witness against her, to gratify his mother, who persecuted the accused. On his introduction into the Forum, at the age of manhood, he gave a largess to the people and a donative to the soldiers: for the pretorian cohorts, he appointed a solemn procession under arms, and marched at the head of them with a shield in his hand; after which he went to return thanks to his father in the senate. Before Claudius, likewise, at the time he was consul, he made a speech for the Bolognese, in Latin, and for the Rhodians and people of Ilium, in Greek. He had the jurisdiction of praefect of the city, for the first time, during the Latin festival; during which the most celebrated advocates brought before him, not short and trifling causes, as is usual in that case, but trials of importance, notwithstanding they had instructions from Claudius himself to the contrary. Soon afterwards, he married Octavia, and exhibited the Circensian games, and hunting of wild beasts, in honour of Claudius.

VIII. He was seventeen years of age at the death of that prince, and as soon as that event was made public, he went out to the cohort on guard between the hours of six and seven; for the omens were so disastrous, that no earlier time of the day was judged proper. On the steps before the palace gate, he was unanimously saluted by the soldiers as their emperor, and then carried in a litter to the camp; thence, after making a short speech to the troops, into the senate-house, where he continued until the evening; of all the immense honours which were heaped upon him, refusing none but the title of FATHER OF HIS COUNTRY, on account of his youth,

IX. He began his reign with an ostentation of dutiful regard to the memory of Claudius, whom he buried with the utmost pomp and magnificence, pronouncing the funeral oration himself, and then had him enrolled amongst the gods. He paid likewise the highest honours to the memory of his father Domitius. He left the management of affairs, both public and private, to his mother. The word which he gave the first day of his reign to the tribune on guard, was, "The Best of Mothers," and afterwards he frequently appeared with her in the streets of Rome in her litter. He settled a colony at Antium, in which he placed the veteran soldiers belonging to the guards; and obliged several of the richest centurions of the first rank to transfer their residence to that place; where he likewise made a noble harbour at a prodigious expense.

X. To establish still further his character, he declared, "that he designed to govern according to the model of Augustus;" and omitted no opportunity of showing his generosity, clemency, and complaisance. The more burthensome taxes he either entirely took off, or diminished. The rewards appointed for informers by the Papian law, he reduced to a fourth part, and distributed to the people four hundred sesterces a man. To the noblest of the senators who were much reduced in their circumstances, he granted annual allowances, in some cases as much as five hundred thousand sesterces; and to the pretorian cohorts a monthly allowance of corn gratis. When called upon to subscribe the sentence, according to custom, of a criminal condemned to die, "I wish," said he, "I had never learnt to read and write." He continually saluted people of the several orders by name, without a prompter. When the senate returned him their thanks for his good government, he replied to them, "It will be time enough to do so when I shall have deserved it." He admitted the common people to see him perform his exercises in the Campus Martius. He frequently declaimed in public, and recited verses of his own composing, not only at home, but in the theatre; so much to the joy of all the people, that public prayers were appointed to be put up to the gods upon that account; and the verses which had been publicly read, were, after being written in gold letters, consecrated to Jupiter Capitolinus.

XI. He presented the people with a great number and variety of spectacles, as the Juvenal and Circensian games, stage-plays, and an exhibition of gladiators. In the Juvenal, he even admitted senators and aged matrons to perform parts. In the Circensian games, he assigned the equestrian order seats apart from the rest of the people, and had races performed by chariots drawn each by four camels. In the games which he instituted for the eternal duration of the empire, and therefore ordered to be called Maximi, many of the senatorian and equestrian order, of both sexes, performed. A distinguished Roman knight descended on the stage by a rope, mounted on an elephant. A Roman play, likewise, composed by Afranius, was brought upon the stage. It was entitled, "The Fire;" and in it the performers were allowed to carry off, and to keep to themselves, the furniture of the house, which, as the plot of the play required, was burnt down in the theatre. Every day during the solemnity, many thousand articles of all descriptions were thrown amongst the people to scramble for; such as fowls of different kinds, tickets for corn, clothes, gold, silver, gems, pearls, pictures, slaves, beasts of burden, wild beasts that had been tamed; at last, ships, lots of houses, and lands, were offered as prizes in a lottery.

XII. These games he beheld from the front of the proscenium. In the show of gladiators, which he exhibited in a wooden amphitheatre, built within a year in the district of the Campus Martius , he ordered that none should be slain, not even the condemned criminals employed in the combats. He secured four hundred senators, and six hundred Roman knights, amongst whom were some of unbroken fortunes and unblemished reputation, to act as gladiators. From the same orders, he engaged persons to encounter wild beasts, and for various other services in the theatre. He presented the public with the representation of a naval fight, upon sea-water, with huge fishes swimming in it; as also with the Pyrrhic dance, performed by certain youths, to each of whom, after the performance was over, he granted the freedom of Rome. During this diversion, a bull covered Pasiphae, concealed within a wooden statue of a cow, as many of the spectators believed. Icarus, upon his first attempt to fly, fell on the stage close to the emperor's pavilion, and bespattered him with blood. For he very seldom presided in the games, but used to view them reclining on a couch, at first through some narrow apertures, but afterwards with the Podium quite open. He was the first who instituted , in imitation of the Greeks, a trial of skill in the three several exercises of music, wrestling, and horse-racing, to be performed at Rome every five years, and which he called Neronia. Upon the dedication of his bath and gymnasium, he furnished the senate and the equestrian order with oil. He appointed as judges of the trial men of consular rank, chosen by lot, who sat with the praetors. At this time he went down into the orchestra amongst the senators, and received the crown for the best performance in Latin prose and verse, for which several persons of the greatest merit contended, but they unanimously yielded to him. The crown for the best performer on the harp, being likewise awarded to him by the judges, he devoutly saluted it, and ordered it to be carried to the statue of Augustus. In the gymnastic exercises, which he presented in the Septa, while they were preparing the great sacrifice of an ox, he shaved his beard for the first time , and putting it up in a casket of gold studded with pearls of great price, consecrated it to Jupiter Capitolinus. He invited the Vestal Virgins to see the wrestlers perform, because, at Olympia, the priestesses of Ceres are allowed the privilege of witnessing that exhibition.

XIII. Amongst the spectacles presented by him, the solemn entrance of Tiridates into the city deserves to be mentioned. This personage, who was king of Armenia, he invited to Rome by very liberal promises. But being prevented by unfavourable weather from showing him to the people upon the day fixed by proclamation, he took the first opportunity which occurred; several cohorts being drawn up under arms, about the temples in the forum, while he was seated on a curule chair on the rostra, in a triumphal dress, amidst the military standards and ensigns. Upon Tiridates advancing towards him, on a stage made shelving for the purpose, he permitted him to throw himself at his feet, but quickly raised him with his right hand, and kissed him. The emperor then, at the king's request, took the turban from his head, and replaced it by a crown, whilst a person of pretorian rank proclaimed in Latin the words in which the prince addressed the emperor as a suppliant. After this ceremony, the king was conducted to the theatre, where, after renewing his obeisance, Nero seated him on his right hand. Being then greeted by universal acclamation with the title of Emperor, and sending his laurel crown to the Capitol, Nero shut the temple of the two-faced Janus, as though there now existed no war throughout the Roman empire.

XIV. He filled the consulship four times : the first for two months, the second and last for six, and the third for four; the two intermediate ones he held successively, but the others after an interval of some years between them.

XV. In the administration of justice, he scarcely ever gave his decision on the pleadings before the next day, and then in writing. His manner of hearing causes was not to allow any adjournment, but to dispatch them in order as they stood. When he withdrew to consult his assessors, he did not debate the matter openly with them; but silently and privately reading over their opinions, which they gave separately in writing, he pronounced sentence from the tribunal according to his own view of the case, as if it was the opinion of the majority. For a long time he would not admit the sons of freedmen into the senate; and those who had been admitted by former princes, he excluded from all public offices. To supernumerary candidates he gave command in the legions, to comfort them under the delay of their hopes. The consulship he commonly conferred for six months; and one of the two consuls dying a little before the first of January, he substituted no one in his place; disliking what had been formerly done for Caninius Rebilus on such an occasion, who was consul for one day only. He allowed the triumphal honours only to those who were of quaestorian rank, and to some of the equestrian order; and bestowed them without regard to military service. And instead of the quaestors, whose office it properly was, he frequently ordered that the addresses, which he sent to the senate on certain occasions, should be read by the consuls.

XVI. He devised a new style of building in the city, ordering piazzas to be erected before all houses, both in the streets and detached, to give facilities from their terraces, in case of fire, for preventing it from spreading; and these he built at his own expense. He likewise designed to extend the city walls as far as Ostia, and bring the sea from thence by a canal into the old city. Many severe regulations and new orders were made in his time. A sumptuary law was enacted. Public suppers were limited to the Sportulae ; and victualling-houses restrained from selling any dressed victuals, except pulse and herbs, whereas before they sold all kinds of meat. He likewise inflicted punishments on the Christians, a sort of people who held a new and impious superstition.

He forbad the revels of the charioteers, who had long assumed a licence to stroll about, and established for themselves a kind of prescriptive right to cheat and thieve, making a jest of it. The partisans of the rival theatrical performers were banished, as well as the actors themselves.

XVII. To prevent forgery, a method was then first invented, of having writings bored, run through three times with a thread, and then sealed. It was likewise provided that in wills, the two first pages, with only the testator's name upon them, should be presented blank to those who were to sign them as witnesses; and that no one who wrote a will for another, should insert any legacy for himself. It was likewise ordained that clients should pay their advocates a certain reasonable fee, but nothing for the court, which was to be gratuitous, the charges for it being paid out of the public treasury; that causes, the cognizance of which before belonged to the judges of the exchequer, should be transferred to the forum, and the ordinary tribunals; and that all appeals from the judges should be made to the senate.

XVIII. He never entertained the least ambition or hope of augmenting and extending the frontiers of the empire. On the contrary, he had thoughts of withdrawing the troops from Britain, and was only restrained from so doing by the fear of appearing to detract from the glory of his father . All that he did was to reduce the kingdom of Pontus, which was ceded to him by Polemon, and also the Alps , upon the death of Cottius, into the form of a province.

XIX. Twice only he undertook any foreign expeditions, one to Alexandria, and the other to Achaia; but he abandoned the prosecution of the former on the very day fixed for his departure, by being deterred both by ill omens, and the hazard of the voyage. For while he was making the circuit of the temples, having seated himself in that of Vesta, when he attempted to rise, the skirt of his robe stuck fast; and he was instantly seized with such a dimness in his eyes, that he could not see a yard before him. In Achaia, he attempted to make a cut through the Isthmus ; and, having made a speech encouraging his pretorians to set about the work, on a signal given by sound of trumpet, he first broke ground with a spade, and carried off a basket full of earth upon his shoulders. He made preparations for an expedition to the Pass of the Caspian mountains ; forming a new legion out of his late levies in Italy, of men all six feet high, which he called the phalanx of Alexander the Great. These transactions, in part unexceptionable, and in part highly commendable, I have brought into one view, in order to separate them from the scandalous and criminal part of his conduct, of which I shall now give an account.

XX. Among the other liberal arts which he was taught in his youth, he was instructed in music; and immediately after his advancement to the empire, he sent for Terpnus, a performer upon the harp , who flourished at that time with the highest reputation. Sitting with him for several days following, as he sang and played after supper, until late at night, he began by degrees to practise upon the instrument himself. Nor did he omit any of those expedients which artists in music adopt, for the preservation and improvement of their voices. He would lie upon his back with a sheet of lead upon his breast, clear his stomach and bowels by vomits and clysters, and forbear the eating of fruits, or food prejudicial to the voice. Encouraged by his proficiency, though his voice was naturally neither loud nor clear, he was desirous of appearing upon the stage, frequently repeating amongst his friends a Greek proverb to this effect: "that no one had any regard for music which they never heard." Accordingly, he made his first public appearance at Naples; and although the theatre quivered with the sudden shock of an earthquake, he did not desist, until he had finished the piece of music he had begun. He played and sung in the same place several times, and for several days together; taking only now and then a little respite to refresh his voice. Impatient of retirement, it was his custom to go from the bath to the theatre; and after dining in the orchestra, amidst a crowded assembly of the people, he promised them in Greek , "that after he had drank a little, he would give them a tune which would make their ears tingle." Being highly pleased with the songs that were sung in his praise by some Alexandrians belonging to the fleet just arrived at Naples , he sent for more of the like singers from Alexandria. At the same time, he chose young men of the equestrian order, and above five thousand robust young fellows from the common people, on purpose to learn various kinds of applause, called bombi, imbrices, and testae , which they were to practise in his favour, whenever he performed. They were divided into several parties, and were remarkable for their fine heads of hair, and were extremely well dressed, with rings upon their left hands. The leaders of these bands had salaries of forty thousand sesterces allowed them.

XXI. At Rome also, being extremely proud of his singing, he ordered the games called Neronia to be celebrated before the time fixed for their return. All now becoming importunate to hear "his heavenly voice," he informed them, "that he would gratify those who desired it at the gardens." But the soldiers then on guard seconding the voice of the people, he promised to comply with their request immediately, and with all his heart. He instantly ordered his name to be entered upon the list of musicians who proposed to contend, and having thrown his lot into the urn among the rest, took his turn, and entered, attended by the prefects of the pretorian cohorts bearing his harp, and followed by the military tribunes, and several of his intimate friends. After he had taken his station, and made the usual prelude, he commanded Cluvius Rufus, a man of consular rank, to proclaim in the theatre, that he intended to sing the story of Niobe. This he accordingly did, and continued it until nearly ten o'clock, but deferred the disposal of the crown, and the remaining part of the solemnity, until the next year; that he might have more frequent opportunities of performing. But that being too long, he could not refrain from often appearing as a public performer during the interval. He made no scruple of exhibiting on the stage, even in the spectacles presented to the people by private persons, and was offered by one of the praetors, no less than a million of sesterces for his services. He likewise sang tragedies in a mask; the visors of the heroes and gods, as also of the heroines and goddesses, being formed into a resemblance of his own face, and that of any woman he was in love with. Amongst the rest, he sung "Canace in Labour," "Orestes the Murderer of his Mother," "Oedipus Blinded," and "Hercules Mad." In the last tragedy, it is said that a young sentinel, posted at the entrance of the stage, seeing him in a prison dress and bound with fetters, as the fable of the play required, ran to his assistance.

XXII. He had from his childhood an extravagant passion for horses; and his constant talk was of the Circensian races, notwithstanding it was prohibited him. Lamenting once, among his fellow-pupils, the case of a charioteer of the green party, who was dragged round the circus at the tail of his chariot, and being reprimanded by his tutor for it, he pretended that he was talking of Hector. In the beginning of his reign, he used to amuse himself daily with chariots drawn by four horses, made of ivory, upon a table. He attended at all the lesser exhibitions in the circus, at first privately, but at last openly; so that nobody ever doubted of his presence on any particular day. Nor did he conceal his desire to have the number of the prizes doubled; so that the races being increased accordingly, the diversion continued until a late hour; the leaders of parties refusing now to bring out their companies for any time less than the whole day. Upon this, he took a fancy for driving the chariot himself, and that even publicly. Having made his first experiment in the gardens, amidst crowds of slaves and other rabble, he at length performed in the view of all the people, in the Circus Maximus, whilst one of his freedmen dropped the napkin in the place where the magistrates used to give the signal. Not satisfied with exhibiting various specimens of his skill in those arts at Rome, he went over to Achaia, as has been already said, principally for this purpose. The several cities, in which solemn trials of musical skill used to be publicly held, had resolved to send him the crowns belonging to those who bore away the prize. These he accepted so graciously, that he not only gave the deputies who brought them an immediate audience, but even invited them to his table. Being requested by some of them to sing at supper, and prodigiously applauded, he said, "the Greeks were the only people who has an ear for music, and were the only good judges of him and his attainments." Without delay he commenced his journey, and on his arrival at Cassiope , exhibited his first musical performance before the altar of Jupiter Cassius.

XXIII. He afterwards appeared at the celebration of all public games in Greece: for such as fell in different years, he brought within the compass of one, and some he ordered to be celebrated a second time in the same year. At Olympia, likewise, contrary to custom, he appointed a public performance in music: and that he might meet with no interruption in this employment, when he was informed by his freedman Helius, that affairs at Rome required his presence, he wrote to him in these words: "Though now all your hopes and wishes are for my speedy return, yet you ought rather to advise and hope that I may come back with a character worthy of Nero." During the time of his musical performance, nobody was allowed to stir out of the theatre upon any account, however necessary; insomuch, that it is said some women with child were delivered there. Many of the spectators being quite wearied with hearing and applauding him, because the town gates were shut, slipped privately over the walls; or counterfeiting themselves dead, were carried out for their funeral. With what extreme anxiety he engaged in these contests, with what keen desire to bear away the prize, and with how much awe of the judges, is scarcely to be believed. As if his adversaries had been on a level with himself, he would watch them narrowly, defame them privately, and sometimes, upon meeting them, rail at them in very scurrilous language; or bribe them, if they were better performers than himself. He always addressed the judges with the most profound reverence before he began, telling them, "he had done all things that were necessary, by way of preparation, but that the issue of the approaching trial was in the hand of fortune; and that they, as wise and skilful men, ought to exclude from their judgment things merely accidental." Upon their encouraging him to have a good heart, he went off with more assurance, but not entirely free from anxiety; interpreting the silence and modesty of some of them into sourness and ill-nature, and saying that he was suspicious of them.

XXIV. In these contests, he adhered so strictly to the rules, that he never durst spit, nor wipe the sweat from his forehead in any other way than with his sleeve. Having, in the performance of a tragedy, dropped his sceptre, and not quickly recovering it, he was in a great fright, lest he should be set aside for the miscarriage, and could not regain his assurance, until an actor who stood by swore he was certain it had not been observed in the midst of the acclamations and exultations of the people. When the prize was adjudged to him, he always proclaimed it himself; and even entered the lists with the heralds. That no memory or the least monument might remain of any other victor in the sacred Grecian games, he ordered all their statues and pictures to be pulled down, dragged away with hooks, and thrown into the common sewers. He drove the chariot with various numbers of horses, and at the Olympic games with no fewer than ten; though, in a poem of his, he had reflected upon Mithridates for that innovation. Being thrown out of his chariot, he was again replaced, but could not retain his seat, and was obliged to give up, before he reached the goal, but was crowned notwithstanding. On his departure, he declared the whole province a free country, and conferred upon the judges in the several games the freedom of Rome, with large sums of money. All these favours he proclaimed himself with his own voice, from the middle of the Stadium, during the solemnity of the Isthmian games.

XXV. On his return from Greece, arriving at Naples, because he had commenced his career as a public performer in that city, he made his entrance in a chariot drawn by white horses through a breach in the city-wall, according to the practice of those who were victorious in the sacred Grecian games. In the same manner he entered Antium, Alba, and Rome. He made his entry into the city riding in the same chariot in which Augustus had triumphed, in a purple tunic, and a cloak embroidered with golden stars, having on his head the crown won at Olympia, and in his right hand that which was given him at the Parthian games: the rest being carried in a procession before him, with inscriptions denoting the places where they had been won, from whom, and in what plays or musical performances; whilst a train followed him with loud acclamations, crying out, that "they were the emperor's attendants, and the soldiers of his triumph." Having then caused an arch of the Circus Maximus to be taken down, he passed through the breach, as also through the Velabrum and the forum, to the Palatine hill and the temple of Apollo. Everywhere as he marched along, victims were slain, whilst the streets were strewed with saffron, and birds, chaplets, and sweetmeats scattered abroad. He suspended the sacred crowns in his chamber, about his beds, and caused statues of himself to be erected in the attire of a harper, and had his likeness stamped upon the coin in the same dress. After this period, he was so far from abating any thing of his application to music, that, for the preservation of his voice, he never addressed the soldiers but by messages, or with some person to deliver his speeches for him, when he thought fit to make his appearance amongst them. Nor did he ever do any thing either in jest or earnest, without a voice-master standing by him to caution him against overstraining his vocal organs, and to apply a handkerchief to his mouth when he did. He offered his friendship, or avowed open enmity to many, according as they were lavish or sparing in giving him their applause.

XXVI. Petulancy, lewdness, luxury, avarice, and cruelty, he practised at first with reserve and in private, as if prompted to them only by the folly of youth; but, even then, the world was of opinion that they were the faults of his nature, and not of his age. After it was dark, he used to enter the taverns disguised in a cap or a wig, and ramble about the streets in sport, which was not void of mischief. He used to beat those he met coming home from supper; and, if they made any resistance, would wound them, and throw them into the common sewer. He broke open and robbed shops; establishing an auction at home for selling his booty. In the scuffles which took place on those occasions, he often ran the hazard of losing his eyes, and even his life; being beaten almost to death by a senator, for handling his wife indecently. After this adventure, he never again ventured abroad at that time of night, without some tribunes following him at a little distance. In the day-time he would be carried to the theatre incognito in a litter, placing himself upon the upper part of the proscenium, where he not only witnessed the quarrels which arose on account of the performances, but also encouraged them. When they came to blows, and stones and pieces of broken benches began to fly about, he threw them plentifully amongst the people, and once even broke a praetor's head.

XXVII. His vices gaining strength by degrees, he laid aside his jocular amusements, and all disguise; breaking out into enormous crimes, without the least attempt to conceal them. His revels were prolonged from mid-day to midnight, while he was frequently refreshed by warm baths, and, in the summer time, by such as were cooled with snow. He often supped in public, in the Naumachia, with the sluices shut, or in the Campus Martius, or the Circus Maximus, being waited upon at table by common prostitutes of the town, and Syrian strumpets and glee-girls. As often as he went down the Tiber to Ostia, or coasted through the gulf of Baiae, booths furnished as brothels and eating-houses, were erected along the shore and river banks; before which stood matrons, who, like bawds and hostesses, allured him to land. It was also his custom to invite himself to supper with his friends; at one of which was expended no less than four millions of sesterces in chaplets, and at another something more in roses.

XXVIII. Besides the abuse of free-born lads, and the debauch of married women, he committed a rape upon Rubria, a Vestal Virgin. He was upon the point of marrying Acte , his freedwoman, having suborned some men of consular rank to swear that she was of royal descent. He gelded the boy Sporus, and endeavoured to transform him into a woman. He even went so far as to marry him, with all the usual formalities of a marriage settlement, the rose-coloured nuptial veil, and a numerous company at the wedding. When the ceremony was over, he had him conducted like a bride to his own house, and treated him as his wife . It was jocularly observed by some person, "that it would have been well for mankind, had such a wife fallen to the lot of his father Domitius." This Sporus he carried about with him in a litter round the

The Lives of the Twelve Caesars - Nero

solemn assemblies and fairs of Greece, and afterwards at Rome through the Sigillaria , dressed in the rich attire of an empress; kissing him from time to time as they rode together. That he entertained an incestuous passion for his mother , but was deterred by her enemies, for fear that this haughty and overbearing woman should, by her compliance, get him entirely into her power, and govern in every thing, was universally believed; especially after he had introduced amongst his concubines a strumpet, who was reported to have a strong resemblance to Agrippina .———

XXIX. He prostituted his own chastity to such a degree, that after he had defiled every part of his person with some unnatural pollution, he at last invented an extraordinary kind of diversion; which was, to be let out of a den in the arena, covered with the skin of a wild beast, and then assail with violence the private parts both of men and women, while they were bound to stakes. After he had vented his furious passion upon them, he finished the play in the embraces of his freedman Doryphorus , to whom he was married in the same way that Sporus had been married to himself; imitating the cries and shrieks of young virgins, when they are ravished. I have been informed from numerous sources, that he firmly believed, no man in the world to be chaste, or any part of his person undefiled; but that most men concealed that vice, and were cunning enough to keep it secret. To those, therefore, who frankly owned their unnatural lewdness, he forgave all other crimes.

XXX. He thought there was no other use of riches and money than to squander them away profusely; regarding all those as sordid wretches who kept their expenses within due bounds; and extolling those as truly noble and generous souls, who lavished away and wasted all they possessed. He praised and admired his uncle Caius , upon no account more, than for squandering in a short time the vast treasure left him by Tiberius. Accordingly, he was himself extravagant and profuse, beyond all bounds. He spent upon Tiridates eight hundred thousand sesterces a day, a sum almost incredible; and at his departure, presented him with upwards of a million . He likewise bestowed upon Menecrates the harper, and Spicillus a gladiator, the estates and houses of men who had received the honour of a triumph. He enriched the usurer Cercopithecus Panerotes with estates both in town and country; and gave him a funeral, in pomp and magnificence little inferior to that of princes. He never wore the same garment twice. He has been known to stake four hundred thousand sesterces on a throw of the dice. It was his custom to fish with a golden net, drawn by silken cords of purple and scarlet. It is said, that he never travelled with less than a thousand baggage-carts; the mules being all shod with silver, and the drivers dressed in scarlet jackets of the finest Canusian cloth , with a numerous train of footmen, and troops of Mazacans , with bracelets on their arms, and mounted upon horses in splendid trappings.

XXXI. In nothing was he more prodigal than in his buildings. He completed his palace by continuing it from the Palatine to the Esquiline hill, calling the building at first only "The Passage," but, after it was burnt down and rebuilt, "The Golden House." Of its dimensions and furniture, it may be sufficient to say thus much: the porch was so high that there stood in it a colossal statue of himself a hundred and twenty feet in height; and the space included in it was so ample, that it had triple porticos a mile in length, and a lake like a sea, surrounded with buildings which had the appearance of a city. Within its area were corn fields, vineyards, pastures, and woods, containing a vast number of animals of various kinds, both wild and tame. In other parts it was entirely over-laid with gold, and adorned with jewels and mother of pearl. The supper rooms were vaulted, and compartments of the ceilings, inlaid with ivory, were made to revolve, and scatter flowers; while they contained pipes which shed unguents upon the guests. The chief banqueting room was circular, and revolved perpetually, night and day, in imitation of the motion of the celestial bodies. The baths were supplied with water from the sea and the Albula. Upon the dedication of this magnificent house after it was finished, all he said in approval of it was, "that he had now a dwelling fit for a man." He commenced making a pond for the reception of all the hot streams from Baiae, which he designed to have continued from Misenum to the Avernian lake, in a conduit, enclosed in galleries; and also a canal from Avernum to Ostia, that ships might pass from one to the other, without a sea voyage. The length of the proposed canal was one hundred and sixty miles; and it was intended to be of breadth sufficient to permit ships with five banks of oars to pass each other. For the execution of these designs, he ordered all prisoners, in every part of the empire, to be brought to Italy; and that even those who were convicted of the most heinous crimes, in lieu of any other sentence, should be condemned to work at them. He was encouraged to all this wild and enormous profusion, not only by the great revenue of the empire, but by the sudden hopes given him of an immense hidden treasure, which queen Dido, upon her flight from Tyre, had brought with her to Africa. This, a Roman knight pretended to assure him, upon good grounds, was still hid there in some deep caverns, and might with a little labour be recovered.

XXXII. But being disappointed in his expectations of this resource, and reduced to such difficulties, for want of money, that he was obliged to defer paying his troops, and the rewards due to the veterans; he resolved upon supplying his necessities by means of false accusations and plunder. In the first place, he ordered, that if any freedman, without sufficient reason, bore the name of the family to which he belonged; the half, instead of three fourths, of his estate should be brought into the exchequer at his decease: also that the estates of all such persons as had not in their wills been mindful of their prince, should be confiscated; and that the lawyers who had drawn or dictated such wills, should be liable to a fine. He ordained likewise, that all words and actions, upon which any informer could ground a prosecution, should be deemed treason. He demanded an equivalent for the crowns which the cities of Greece had at any time offered him in the solemn games. Having forbad any one to use the colours of amethyst and Tyrian purple, he privately sent a person to sell a few ounces of them upon the day of the Nundinae, and then shut up all the merchants' shops, on the pretext that his edict had been violated. It is said, that, as he was playing and singing in the theatre, observing a married lady dressed in the purple which he had prohibited, he pointed her out to his procurators; upon which she was immediately dragged out of her seat, and not only stripped of her clothes, but her property. He never nominated a person to any office without saying to him, "You know what I want; and let us take care that nobody has any thing he can call his own." At last he rifled many temples of the rich offerings with which they were stored, and melted down all the gold and silver statues, and amongst them those of the penates , which Galba afterwards restored.

XXXIII. He began the practice of parricide and murder with Claudius himself; for although he was not the contriver of his death, he was privy to the plot. Nor did he make any secret of it; but used afterwards to commend, in a Greek proverb, mushrooms as food fit for the gods, because Claudius had been poisoned with them. He traduced his memory both by word and deed in the grossest manner; one while charging him with folly, another while with cruelty. For he used to say by way of jest, that he had ceased morari amongst men, pronouncing the first syllable long; and treated as null many of his decrees and ordinances, as made by a doting old blockhead. He enclosed the place where his body was burnt with only a low wall of rough masonry. He attempted to poison Britannicus, as much out of envy because he had a sweeter voice, as from apprehension of what might ensue from the respect which the people entertained for his father's memory. He employed for this purpose a woman named Locusta, who had been a witness against some persons guilty of like practices. But the poison she gave him, working more slowly than he expected, and only causing a purge, he sent for the woman, and beat her with his own hand, charging her with administering an antidote instead of poison; and upon her alleging in excuse, that she had given Britannicus but a gentle mixture in order to prevent suspicion, "Think you," said he, "that I am afraid of the Julian law;" and obliged her to prepare, in his own chamber and before his eyes, as quick and strong a dose as possible. This he tried upon a kid: but the animal lingering for five hours before it expired, he ordered her to go to work again; and when she had done, he gave the poison to a pig, which dying immediately, he commanded the potion to be brought into the eating-room and given to Britannicus, while he was at supper with him. The prince had no sooner tasted it than he sunk on the floor, Nero meanwhile, pretending to the guests, that it was only a fit of the falling sickness, to which, he said, he was subject. He buried him the following day, in a mean and hurried way, during violent storms of rain. He gave Locusta a pardon, and rewarded her with a great estate in land, placing some disciples with her, to be instructed in her trade.

XXXIV. His mother being used to make strict inquiry into what he said or did, and to reprimand him with the freedom of a parent, he was so much offended, that he endeavoured to expose her to public resentment, by frequently pretending a resolution to quit the government, and retire to Rhodes. Soon afterwards, he deprived her of all honour and power, took from her the guard of Roman and German soldiers, banished her from the palace and from his society, and persecuted her in every way he could contrive; employing persons to harass her when at Rome with law-suits, and to disturb her in her retirement from town with the most scurrilous and abusive language, following her about by land and sea. But being terrified with her menaces and violent spirit, he resolved upon her destruction, and thrice attempted it by poison. Finding, however, that she had previously secured herself by antidotes, he contrived machinery, by which the floor over her bed-chamber might be made to fall upon her while she was asleep in the night. This design miscarrying likewise, through the little caution used by those who were in the secret, his next stratagem was to construct a ship which could be easily shivered, in hopes of destroying her either by drowning, or by the deck above her cabin crushing her in its fall. Accordingly, under colour of a pretended reconciliation, he wrote her an extremely affectionate letter, inviting her to Baiae, to celebrate with him the festival of Minerva. He had given private orders to the captains of the galleys which were to attend her, to shatter to pieces the ship in which she had come, by falling foul of it, but in such manner that it might appear to be done accidentally. He prolonged the entertainment, for the more convenient opportunity of executing the plot in the night; and at her return for Bauli , instead of the old ship which had conveyed her to Baiae, he offered that which he had contrived for her destruction. He attended her to the vessel in a very cheerful mood, and, at parting with her, kissed her breasts; after which he sat up very late in the night, waiting with great anxiety to learn the issue of his project. But receiving information that every thing had fallen out contrary to his wish, and that she had saved herself by swimming,—not knowing what course to take, upon her freedman, Lucius Agerinus bringing word, with great joy, that she was safe and well, he privately dropped a poniard by him. He then commanded the freedman to be seized and put in chains, under pretence of his having been employed by his mother to assassinate him; at the same time ordering her to be put to death, and giving out, that, to avoid punishment for her intended crime, she had laid violent hands upon herself. Other circumstances, still more horrible, are related on good authority; as that he went to view her corpse, and handling her limbs, pointed out some blemishes, and commended other points; and that, growing thirsty during the survey, he called for drink. Yet he was never afterwards able to bear the stings of his own conscience for this atrocious act, although encouraged by the congratulatory addresses of the army, the senate, and people. He frequently affirmed that he was haunted by his mother's ghost, and persecuted with the whips and burning torches of the Furies. Nay, he attempted by magical rites to bring up her ghost from below, and soften her rage against him. When he was in Greece, he durst not attend the celebration of the Eleusinian mysteries, at the initiation of which, impious and wicked persons are warned by the voice of the herald from approaching the rites . Besides the murder of his mother, he had been guilty of that of his aunt; for, being obliged to keep her bed in consequence of a complaint in her bowels, he paid her a visit, and she, being then advanced in years, stroking his downy chin, in the tenderness of affection, said to him: "May I but live to see the day when this is shaved for the first time , and I shall then die contented." He turned, however, to those about him, made a jest of it, saying, that he would have his beard immediately taken off, and ordered the physicians to give her more violent purgatives. He seized upon her estate before she had expired; suppressing her will, that he might enjoy the whole himself.

XXXV. He had, besides Octavia, two other wives: Poppaea Sabina, whose father had borne the office of quaestor, and who had been married before to a Roman knight: and, after her, Statilia Messalina, great-grand-daughter of Taurus who was twice consul, and received the honour of a triumph. To obtain possession of her, he put to death her husband, Atticus Vestinus, who was then consul. He soon became disgusted with Octavia, and ceased from having any intercourse with her; and being censured by his friends for it, he replied, "She ought to be satisfied with having the rank and appendages of his wife." Soon afterwards, he made several attempts, but in vain, to strangle her, and then divorced her for barrenness. But the people, disapproving of the divorce, and making severe comments upon it, he also banished her . At last he put her to death, upon a charge of adultery, so impudent and false, that, when all those who were put to the torture positively denied their knowledge of it, he suborned his pedagogue, Anicetus, to affirm, that he had secretly intrigued with and debauched her. He married Poppaea twelve days after the divorce of Octavia , and entertained a great affection for her; but, nevertheless, killed her with a kick which he gave her when she was big with child, and in bad health, only because she found fault with him for returning late from driving his chariot. He had by her a daughter, Claudia Augusta, who died an infant. There was no person at all connected with him who escaped his deadly and unjust cruelty. Under pretence of her being engaged in a plot against him, he put to death Antonia, Claudius's daughter, who refused to marry him after the death of Poppaea. In the same way, he destroyed all who were allied to him either by blood or marriage; amongst whom was young Aulus Plautinus. He first compelled him to submit to his unnatural lust, and then ordered him to be executed, crying out, "Let my mother bestow her kisses on my successor thus defiled;" pretending that he had been his mothers paramour, and by her encouraged to aspire to the empire. His step-son, Rufinus Crispinus, Poppaea's son, though a minor, he ordered to be drowned in the sea, while he was fishing, by his own slaves, because he was reported to act frequently amongst his play-fellows the part of a general or an emperor. He banished Tuscus, his nurse's son, for presuming, when he was procurator of Egypt, to wash in the baths which had been constructed in expectation of his own coming. Seneca, his preceptor, he forced to kill himself , though, upon his desiring leave to retire, and offering to surrender his estate, he solemnly swore, "that there was no foundation for his suspicions, and that he would perish himself sooner than hurt him." Having promised Burrhus, the praetorian prefect, a remedy for a swelling in his throat, he sent him poison. Some old

The Lives of the Twelve Caesars - Nero

rich freedmen of Claudius, who had formerly not only promoted his adoption, but were also instrumental to his advancement to the empire, and had been his governors, he took off by poison given them in their meat or drink.

XXXVI. Nor did he proceed with less cruelty against those who were not of his family. A blazing star, which is vulgarly supposed to portend destruction to kings and princes, appeared above the horizon several nights successively . He felt great anxiety on account of this phenomenon, and being informed by one Babilus, an astrologer, that princes were used to expiate such omens by the sacrifice of illustrious persons, and so avert the danger foreboded to their own persons, by bringing it on the heads of their chief men, he resolved on the destruction of the principal nobility in Rome. He was the more encouraged to this, because he had some plausible pretence for carrying it into execution, from the discovery of two conspiracies against him; the former and more dangerous of which was that formed by Piso , and discovered at Rome; the other was that of Vinicius , at Beneventum. The conspirators were brought to their trials loaded with triple fetters. Some ingenuously confessed the charge; others avowed that they thought the design against his life an act of favour for which he was obliged to them, as it was impossible in any other way than by death to relieve a person rendered infamous by crimes of the greatest enormity. The children of those who had been condemned, were banished the city, and afterwards either poisoned or starved to death. It is asserted that some of them, with their tutors, and the slaves who carried their satchels, were all poisoned together at one dinner; and others not suffered to seek their daily bread.

XXXVII. From this period he butchered, without distinction or quarter, all whom his caprice suggested as objects for his cruelty; and upon the most frivolous pretences. To mention only a few: Salvidienus Orfitus was accused of letting out three taverns attached to his house in the Forum to some cities for the use of their deputies at Rome. The charge against Cassius Longinus, a lawyer who had lost his sight, was, that he kept amongst the busts of his ancestors that of Caius Cassius, who was concerned in the death of Julius Caesar. The only charge objected against Paetus Thrasea was, that he had a melancholy cast of features, and looked like a schoolmaster. He allowed but one hour to those whom he obliged to kill themselves; and, to prevent delay, he sent them physicians "to cure them immediately, if they lingered beyond that time;" for so he called bleeding them to death. There was at that time an Egyptian of a most voracious appetite, who would digest raw flesh, or any thing else that was given him. It was credibly reported, that the emperor was extremely desirous of furnishing him with living men to tear and devour. Being elated with his great success in the perpetration of crimes, he declared, "that no prince before himself ever knew the extent of his power." He threw out strong intimations that he would not even spare the senators who survived, but would entirely extirpate that order, and put the provinces and armies into the hands of the Roman knights and his own freedmen. It is certain that he never gave or vouchsafed to allow any one the customary kiss, either on entering or departing, or even returned a salute. And at the inauguration of a work, the cut through the Isthmus , he, with a loud voice, amidst the assembled multitude, uttered a prayer, that "the undertaking might prove fortunate for himself and the Roman people," without taking the smallest notice of the senate.

XXXVIII. He spared, moreover, neither the people of Rome, nor the capital of his country. Somebody in conversation saying—

Emou thanontos gaia michthaeto pyri
When I am dead let fire devour the world—

"Nay," said he, "let it be while I am living" [emou xontos]. And he acted accordingly: for, pretending to be disgusted with the old buildings, and the narrow and winding streets, he set the city on fire so openly, that many of consular rank caught his own household servants on their property with tow, and torches in their hands, but durst not meddle with them. There being near his Golden House some granaries, the site of which he exceedingly coveted, they were battered as if with machines of war, and set on fire, the walls being built of stone. During six days and seven nights this terrible devastation continued, the people being obliged to fly to the tombs and monuments for lodging and shelter. Meanwhile, a vast number of stately buildings, the houses of generals celebrated in former times, and even then still decorated with the spoils of war, were laid in ashes; as well as the temples of the gods, which had been vowed and dedicated by the kings of Rome, and afterwards in the Punic and Gallic wars: in short, everything that was remarkable and worthy to be seen which time had spared . This fire he beheld from a tower in the house of Mecaenas, and "being greatly delighted," as he said, "with the beautiful effects of the conflagration," he sung a poem on the ruin of Troy, in the tragic dress he used on the stage. To turn this calamity to his own advantage by plunder and rapine, he promised to remove the bodies of those who had perished in the fire, and clear the rubbish at his own expense; suffering no one to meddle with the remains of their property. But he not only received, but exacted contributions on account of the loss, until he had exhausted the means both of the provinces and private persons.

XXXIX. To these terrible and shameful calamities brought upon the people by their prince, were added some proceeding from misfortune. Such were a pestilence, by which, within the space of one autumn, there died no less than thirty thousand persons, as appeared from the registers in the temple of Libitina; a great disaster in Britain , where two of the principal towns belonging to the Romans were plundered; and a dreadful havoc made both amongst our troops and allies; a shameful discomfiture of the army of the East; where, in Armenia, the legions were obliged to pass under the yoke, and it was with great difficulty that Syria was retained. Amidst all these disasters, it was strange, and, indeed, particularly remarkable, that he bore nothing more patiently than the scurrilous language and railing abuse which was in every one's mouth; treating no class of persons with more gentleness, than those who assailed him with invective and lampoons. Many things of that kind were posted up about the city, or otherwise published, both in Greek and Latin: such as these,

> Neron, Orestaes, Alkmaion, maetroktonai.
> Neonymphon Neron, idian maeter apekteinen.

> Orestes and Alcaeon—Nero too,
> The lustful Nero, worst of all the crew,
> Fresh from his bridal—their own mothers slew.

> Quis neget Aeneae magna de stirpe Neronem?
> Sustulit hic matrem: sustulit ille patrem.

> Sprung from Aeneas, pious, wise and great,
> Who says that Nero is degenerate?
> Safe through the flames, one bore his sire; the other,
> To save himself, took off his loving mother.

> Dum tendit citharam noster, dum cornua Parthus,
> Noster erit Paean, ille Ekataebeletaes.
> His lyre to harmony our Nero strings;

His arrows o'er the plain the Parthian wings:
Ours call the tuneful Paean,—famed in war,
The other Phoebus name, the god who shoots afar.

Roma domus fiet: Vejos migrate, Quirites,
Si non et Vejos occupat ista domus.

All Rome will be one house: to Veii fly,
Should it not stretch to Veii, by and by.

But he neither made any inquiry after the authors, nor when information was laid before the senate against some of them, would he allow a severe sentence to be passed. Isidorus, the Cynic philosopher, said to him aloud, as he was passing along the streets, "You sing the misfortunes of Nauplius well, but behave badly yourself." And Datus, a comic actor, when repeating these words in the piece, "Farewell, father! Farewell mother!" mimicked the gestures of persons drinking and swimming, significantly alluding to the deaths of Claudius and Agrippina: and on uttering the last clause,

Orcus vobis ducit pedes;
You stand this moment on the brink of Orcus;

he plainly intimated his application of it to the precarious position of the senate. Yet Nero only banished the player and philosopher from the city and Italy; either because he was insensible to shame, or from apprehension that if he discovered his vexation, still keener things might be said of him.

XL. The world, after tolerating such an emperor for little less than fourteen years, at length forsook him; the Gauls, headed by Julius Vindex, who at that time governed the province as pro-praetor, being the first to revolt. Nero had been formerly told by astrologers, that it would be his fortune to be at last deserted by all the world; and this occasioned that celebrated saying of his, "An artist can live in any country;" by which he meant to offer as an excuse for his practice of music, that it was not only his amusement as a prince, but might be his support when reduced to a private station. Yet some of the astrologers promised him, in his forlorn state, the rule of the East, and some in express words the kingdom of Jerusalem. But the greater part of them flattered him with assurances of his being restored to his former fortune. And being most inclined to believe the latter prediction, upon losing Britain and

Armenia, he imagined he had run through all the misfortunes which the fates had decreed him. But when, upon consulting the oracle of Apollo at Delphi, he was advised to beware of the seventy-third year, as if he were not to die till then, never thinking of Galba's age, he conceived such hopes, not only of living to advanced years, but of constant and singular good fortune, that having lost some things of great value by shipwreck, he scrupled not to say amongst his friends, that "the fishes would bring them back to him." At Naples he heard of the insurrection in Gaul, on the anniversary of the day on which he killed his mother, and bore it with so much unconcern, as to excite a suspicion that he was really glad of it, since he had now a fair opportunity of plundering those wealthy provinces by the right of war. Immediately going to the gymnasium, he witnessed the exercise of the wrestlers with the greatest delight. Being interrupted at supper with letters which brought yet worse news, he expressed no greater resentment, than only to threaten the rebels. For eight days together, he never attempted to answer any letters, nor give any orders, but buried the whole affair in profound silence.

XLI. Being roused at last by numerous proclamations of Vindex, treating him with reproaches and contempt, he in a letter to the senate exhorted them to avenge his wrongs and those of the republic; desiring them to excuse his not appearing in the senate-house, because he had got cold. But nothing so much galled him, as to find himself railed at as a pitiful harper, and, instead of Nero, styled Aenobarbus: which being his family name, since he was upbraided with it, he declared that he would resume it, and lay aside the name he had taken by adoption. Passing by the other accusations as wholly groundless, he earnestly refuted that of his want of skill in an art upon which he had bestowed so much pains, and in which he had arrived at such perfection; asking frequently those about him, "if they knew any one who was a more accomplished musician?" But being alarmed by messengers after messengers of ill news from Gaul, he returned in great consternation to Rome. On the road, his mind was somewhat relieved, by observing the frivolous omen of a Gaulish soldier defeated and dragged by the hair by a Roman knight, which was sculptured on a monument; so that he leaped for joy, and adored the heavens. Even then he made no appeal either to the senate or people, but calling together some of the leading men at his own house, he held a hasty consultation upon the present state of affairs, and then, during the remainder of the day, carried them about with him to view some musical instruments, of a new invention, which were played by water exhibiting all the parts, and discoursing upon the principles and difficulties of the contrivance; which, he told them, he intended to produce in the theatre, if Vindex would give him leave.

XLII. Soon afterwards, he received intelligence that Galba and the Spaniards had declared against him; upon which, he fainted, and losing his reason, lay a long time speechless, apparently dead. As soon as recovered from this state stupefaction he tore his clothes, and beat his head, crying out, "It is all over with me!" His nurse endeavouring to comfort him, and telling him that the like things had happened to other princes before him, he replied, "I am beyond all example wretched, for I have lost an empire whilst I am still living." He, nevertheless, abated nothing of his luxury and inattention to business. Nay, on the arrival of good news from the provinces, he, at a sumptuous entertainment, sung with an air of merriment, some jovial verses upon the leaders of the revolt, which were made public; and accompanied them with suitable gestures. Being carried privately to the theatre, he sent word to an actor who was applauded by the spectators, "that he had it all his own way, now that he himself did not appear on the stage."

XLIII. At the first breaking out of these troubles, it is believed that he had formed many designs of a monstrous nature, although conformable enough to his natural disposition. These were to send new governors and commanders to the provinces and the armies, and employ assassins to butcher all the former governors and commanders, as men unanimously engaged in a conspiracy against him; to massacre the exiles in every quarter, and all the Gaulish population in Rome; the former lest they should join the insurrection; the latter as privy to the designs of their countrymen, and ready to support them; to abandon Gaul itself, to be wasted and plundered by his armies; to poison the whole senate at a feast; to fire the city, and then let loose the wild beasts upon the people, in order to impede their stopping the progress of the flames. But being deterred from the execution of these designs not so much by remorse of conscience, as by despair of being able to effect them, and judging an expedition into Gaul necessary, he removed the consuls from their office, before the time of its expiration was arrived; and in their room assumed the consulship himself without a colleague, as if the fates had decreed that Gaul should not be conquered, but by a consul. Upon assuming the fasces, after an entertainment at the palace, as he walked out of the room leaning on the arms of some of his friends, he declared, that as soon as he arrived in the province, he would make his appearance amongst the troops, unarmed, and do nothing but weep: and that, after he had brought the mutineers to repentance, he would, the next day, in the public rejoicings, sing songs of triumph, which he must now, without loss of time, apply himself to compose.

XLIV. In preparing for this expedition, his first care was to provide carriages for his musical instruments and machinery to be used upon the stage; to have the hair of the concubines he carried with him dressed in the fashion of men; and to supply them with battle-axes, and Amazonian bucklers. He summoned the city-tribes to enlist; but no qualified persons appearing, he ordered all masters to send a certain number of slaves, the best they had, not excepting their stewards and secretaries. He commanded the several orders of the people to bring in a fixed proportion of their estates, as they stood in the censor's books; all tenants of houses and mansions to pay one year's rent forthwith into the exchequer; and, with unheard-of strictness, would receive only new coin of the purest silver and the finest gold; insomuch that most people refused to pay, crying out unanimously that he ought to squeeze the informers, and oblige them to surrender their gains.

XLV. The general odium in which he was held received an increase by the great scarcity of corn, and an occurrence connected with it. For, as it happened just at that time, there arrived from Alexandria a ship, which was said to be freighted with dust for the wrestlers belonging to the emperor. This so much inflamed the public rage, that he was treated with the utmost abuse and scurrility. Upon the top of one of his statues was placed the figure of a chariot with a Greek inscription, that "Now indeed he had a race to run; let him be gone." A little bag was tied about another, with a ticket containing these words; "What could I do?"—"Truly thou hast merited the sack." Some person likewise wrote on the pillars in the forum, "that he had even woke the cocks with his singing." And many, in the night-time, pretending to find fault with their servants, frequently called for a Vindex.

XLVI. He was also terrified with manifest warnings, both old and new, arising from dreams, auspices, and omens. He had never been used to dream before the murder of his mother. After that event, he fancied in his sleep that he was steering a ship, and that the rudder was forced from him: that he was dragged by his wife Octavia into a prodigiously dark place; and was at one time covered over with a vast swarm of winged ants, and at another, surrounded by the national images which were set up near Pompey's theatre, and hindered from advancing farther; that a Spanish jennet he was fond of, had his hinder parts so changed, as to resemble those of an ape; and having his head only left unaltered, neighed very harmoniously. The doors of the mausoleum of Augustus flying open of themselves, there issued from it a voice, calling on him by name. The Lares being adorned with fresh garlands on the calends (the first) of January, fell down during the preparations for sacrificing to them. While he was taking the omens, Sporus presented him with a ring, the stone of which had carved upon it the Rape of Proserpine. When a great multitude of the several orders was assembled, to attend at the solemnity of making vows to the gods, it was a long time before the keys of the Capitol could be found. And when, in a speech of his to the senate against Vindex, these words were read, "that the miscreants should be punished and soon make the end they merited," they all cried out, "You will do it, Augustus." It was likewise remarked, that the last tragic piece which he sung, was Oedipus in Exile, and that he fell as he was repeating this verse:

>Thanein m' anoge syngamos, maetaer, pataer.
>Wife, mother, father, force me to my end.

XLVII. Meanwhile, on the arrival of the news, that the rest of the armies had declared against him, he tore to pieces the letters which were delivered to him at dinner, overthrew the table, and dashed with violence against the ground two favourite cups, which he called Homer's, because some of that poet's verses were cut upon them. Then taking from Locusta a dose of poison, which he put up in a golden box, he went into the Servilian gardens, and thence dispatching a trusty freedman to Ostia, with orders to make ready a fleet, he endeavoured to prevail with some tribunes and centurions of the pretorian guards to attend him in his flight; but part of them showing no great inclination to comply, others absolutely refusing, and one of them crying out aloud,

>Usque adeone mori miserum est?
>Say, is it then so sad a thing to die?

he was in great perplexity whether he should submit himself to Galba, or apply to the Parthians for protection, or else appear before the people dressed in mourning, and, upon the rostra, in the most piteous manner, beg pardon for his past misdemeanors, and, if he could not prevail, request of them to grant him at least the government of Egypt. A speech to this purpose was afterwards found in his writing-case. But it is conjectured that he durst not venture upon this project, for fear of being torn to pieces, before he could get to the Forum. Deferring, therefore, his resolution until the next day, he awoke about midnight, and finding the guards withdrawn, he leaped out of bed, and sent round for his friends. But none of them vouchsafing any message in reply, he went with a few attendants to their houses. The doors being every where shut, and no one giving him any answer, he returned to his bed-chamber; whence those who had the charge of it had all now eloped; some having gone one way, and some another, carrying off with them his bedding and box of poison. He then endeavoured to find Spicillus, the gladiator, or some one to kill him; but not being able to procure any one, "What!" said he, "have I then neither friend nor foe?" and immediately ran out, as if he would throw himself into the Tiber.

XLVIII. But this furious impulse subsiding, he wished for some place of privacy, where he might collect his thoughts; and his freedman Phaon offering him his country-house, between the Salarian and Nomentan roads, about four miles from the city, he mounted a horse, barefoot as he was, and in his tunic, only slipping over it an old soiled cloak; with his head muffled up, and an handkerchief before his face, and four persons only to attend him, of whom Sporus was one. He was suddenly struck with horror by an earthquake, and by a flash of lightning which darted full in his face, and heard from the neighbouring camp the shouts of the soldiers, wishing his destruction, and prosperity to Galba. He also heard a traveller they met on the road, say, "They are in pursuit of Nero:" and another ask, "Is there any news in the city about Nero?" Uncovering his face when his horse was started by the scent of a carcase which lay in the road, he was recognized and saluted by an old soldier who had been discharged from the guards. When they came to the lane which turned up to the house, they quitted their horses, and with much difficulty he wound among bushes, and briars, and along a track through a bed of rushes, over which they spread their cloaks for him to walk on. Having reached a wall at the back of the villa, Phaon advised him to hide himself awhile in a sand-pit; when he replied, "I will not go under-ground alive." Staying there some little time, while preparations were made for bringing him privately into the villa, he took up some water out of a neighbouring tank in his hand, to drink, saying, "This is Nero's distilled water." Then his cloak having been torn by the brambles, he pulled out the thorns which stuck in it. At last, being admitted, creeping upon his hands and knees, through a hole made for him in the wall, he lay down in the first closet he came to, upon a miserable pallet, with an old coverlet thrown over it; and being both hungry and thirsty, though he refused some coarse bread that was brought him, he drank a little warm water.

XLIX. All who surrounded him now pressing him to save himself from the indignities which were ready to befall him, he ordered a pit to be sunk before his eyes, of the size of his body, and the bottom to be covered with pieces of marble put together, if any could be found about the house; and water and wood , to be got ready for immediate use about his corpse; weeping at every thing that was done, and frequently saying, "What an artist is now about to perish!" Meanwhile, letters being brought in by a servant belonging to Phaon, he snatched them out of his hand, and there read, "That he had been declared an enemy by the senate, and that search was making for him, that he might be punished according to the ancient custom of the Romans." He then inquired what kind of punishment that was; and being told, that the practice was to strip the criminal naked, and scourge him to death, while his neck was fastened within a forked stake, he was so terrified that he took up two daggers which he had brought with him, and after feeling the points of both, put them up again, saying, "The fatal hour is not yet come." One while, he begged of Sporus to begin to wail and lament; another while, he entreated that one of them would set him an example by killing himself; and then again, he condemned his own want of resolution in these words: "I yet live to my shame and disgrace: this is not becoming for Nero: it is not becoming. Thou oughtest in such circumstances to have a good heart: Come, then: courage, man!" The horsemen who had received orders to bring him away alive, were now approaching the house. As soon as he heard them coming, he uttered with a trembling voice the following verse,

> Hippon m' okupodon amphi ktupos ouata ballei;
> The noise of swift-heel'd steeds assails my ears;

he drove a dagger into his throat, being assisted in the act by Epaphroditus, his secretary. A centurion bursting in just as he was half-dead, and applying his cloak to the wound, pretending that he was come to his assistance, he made no other reply but this, "'Tis too late;" and "Is this your loyalty?" Immediately after pronouncing these words, he expired, with his eyes fixed and starting out of his head, to the terror of all who beheld him. He had requested of his attendants, as the most essential favour, that they would let no one have his head, but that by all means his body might be burnt entire. And this, Icelus, Galba's freedman, granted. He had but a little before been discharged from the prison into which he had been thrown, when the disturbances first broke out.

L. The expenses of his funeral amounted to two hundred thousand sesterces; the bed upon which his body was carried to the pile and burnt, being covered with the white robes, interwoven with gold, which he had worn upon the calends of January preceding. His nurses, Ecloge and Alexandra, with his concubine Acte, deposited his remains in the tomb belonging to the family of the Domitii, which stands upon the top of the Hill of the Gardens, and is to be seen from the Campus Martius. In that monument, a coffin of porphyry, with an altar of marble of Luna over it, is enclosed by a wall built of stone brought from Thasos.

LI. In stature he was a little below the common height; his skin was foul and spotted; his hair inclined to yellow; his features were agreeable, rather than handsome; his eyes grey and dull, his neck was thick, his belly prominent, his legs very slender, his constitution sound. For, though excessively luxurious in his mode of living, he had, in the course of fourteen years, only three fits of sickness; which were so slight, that he neither forbore the use of wine, nor made any alteration in his usual diet. In his dress, and the care of his person, he was so careless, that he had his hair cut in rings, one above another; and when in Achaia, he let it grow long behind; and he generally appeared in public in the loose dress which he used at table, with a handkerchief about his neck, and without either a girdle or shoes.

LII. He was instructed, when a boy, in the rudiments of almost all the liberal sciences; but his mother diverted him from the study of philosophy, as unsuited to one destined to be an emperor; and his preceptor, Seneca, discouraged him from reading the ancient orators, that he might longer secure his devotion to himself. Therefore, having a turn for poetry, he composed verses both with pleasure and ease; nor did he, as some think, publish those of other writers as his own. Several little pocket-books and loose sheets have cone into my possession, which contain some well-known verses in his own hand, and written in such a manner, that it was very evident, from the blotting and interlining, that they had not been transcribed from a copy, nor dictated by another, but were written by the composer of them.

LIII. He had likewise great taste for drawing and painting, as well as for moulding statues in plaster. But, above all things, he most eagerly coveted popularity, being the rival of every man who obtained the applause of the people for any thing he did. It was the general belief, that, after the crowns he won by his performances on the stage, he would the next lustrum have taken his place among the wrestlers at the Olympic games. For he was continually practising that art; nor did he witness the gymnastic games in any part of

Greece otherwise than sitting upon the ground in the stadium, as the umpires do. And if a pair of wrestlers happened to break the bounds, he would with his own hands drag them back into the centre of the circle. Because he was thought to equal Apollo in music, and the sun in chariot-driving, he resolved also to imitate the achievements of Hercules. And they say that a lion was got ready for him to kill, either with a club, or with a close hug, in view of the people in the amphitheatre; which he was to perform naked.

LIV. Towards the end of his life, he publicly vowed, that if his power in the state was securely re-established, he would, in the spectacles which he intended to exhibit in honour of his success, include a performance upon organs , as well as upon flutes and bagpipes, and, on the last day of the games, would act in the play, and take the part of Turnus, as we find it in Virgil. And there are some who say, that he put to death the player Paris as a dangerous rival.

LV. He had an insatiable desire to immortalize his name, and acquire a reputation which should last through all succeeding ages; but it was capriciously directed. He therefore took from several things and places their former appellations, and gave them new names derived from his own. He called the month of April, Neroneus, and designed changing the name of Rome into that of Neropolis.

LVI. He held all religious rites in contempt, except those of the Syrian Goddess ; but at last he paid her so little reverence, that he made water upon her; being now engaged in another superstition, in which only he obstinately persisted. For having received from some obscure plebeian a little image of a girl, as a preservative against plots, and discovering a conspiracy immediately after, he constantly worshipped his imaginary protectress as the greatest amongst the gods, offering to her three sacrifices daily. He was also desirous to have it supposed that he had, by revelations from this deity, a knowledge of future events. A few months before he died, he attended a sacrifice, according to the Etruscan rites, but the omens were not favourable.

LVII. He died in the thirty-second year of his age , upon the same day on which he had formerly put Octavia to death; and the public joy was so great upon the occasion, that the common people ran about the city with caps upon their heads. Some, however, were not wanting, who for a long time decked his tomb with spring and summer flowers. Sometimes they placed his image upon the rostra, dressed in robes of state; at another, they published proclamations in his name, as if he were still alive, and would shortly return to Rome, and take vengeance on all his enemies. Vologesus, king of the Parthians, when he sent ambassadors to the senate to renew his alliance with the Roman people, earnestly requested that due honour should be paid to the memory of Nero; and, to conclude, when, twenty years afterwards, at which time I was a young man, some person of obscure birth gave himself out for Nero, that name secured him so favourable a reception from the Parthians, that he was very zealously supported, and it was with much difficulty that they were prevailed upon to give him up.

Though no law had ever passed for regulating the transmission of the imperial power, yet the design of conveying it by lineal descent was implied in the practice of adoption. By the rule of hereditary succession, Britannicus, the son of Claudius, was the natural heir to the throne; but he was supplanted by the artifices of his stepmother, who had the address to procure it for her own son, Nero. From the time of Augustus it had been the custom of each of the new sovereigns to commence his reign in such a manner as tended to acquire popularity, however much they all afterwards degenerated from those specious beginnings. Whether this proceeded entirely from policy, or that nature was not yet vitiated by the intoxication of uncontrolled power, is uncertain; but such were the excesses into which they afterwards plunged, that we can scarcely exempt any of them, except, perhaps, Claudius, from the imputation of great original depravity. The vicious temper of Tiberius was known to his own mother, Livia; that of Caligula had been obvious to those about him from his infancy; Claudius seems to have had naturally a stronger tendency to weakness than to vice; but the inherent wickedness of Nero was discovered at an early period by his preceptor, Seneca. Yet even this emperor commenced his reign in a manner which procured him approbation. Of all the Roman emperors who had hitherto reigned, he seems to have been most corrupted by profligate favourites, who flattered his follies and vices, to promote their own aggrandisement. In the number of these was Tigellinus, who met at last with the fate which he had so amply merited.

The several reigns from the death of Augustus present us with uncommon scenes of cruelty and horror; but it was reserved for that of Nero to exhibit to the world the atrocious act of an emperor deliberately procuring the death of his mother.

Julia Agrippina was the daughter of Germanicus, and married Domitius Aenobarbus, by whom she had Nero. At the death of Messalina she was a widow; and Claudius, her uncle, entertaining a design of entering again into the married state, she aspired to an incestuous alliance with him, in competition with Lollia Paulina, a woman of beauty and intrigue, who had been married to C. Caesar. The two rivals were strongly supported by their respective parties; but Agrippina, by her superior interest with the emperor's favourites, and the familiarity to which her near relation gave her a claim, obtained the preference; and the portentous nuptials of the emperor and his niece were publicly solemnized in the palace. Whether she was prompted to this flagrant indecency by personal ambition alone, or by the desire of procuring the succession to the empire for her son, is uncertain; but there remains no doubt of her having removed Claudius by poison, with a view to the object now mentioned. Besides Claudius, she projected the death of L. Silanus, and she accomplished that of his brother, Junius Silanus, by means likewise of poison. She appears to have been richly endowed with the gifts of nature, but in her disposition intriguing, violent, imperious, and ready to sacrifice every principle of virtue, in the pursuit of supreme power or sensual gratification. As she resembled Livia in the ambition of a mother, and the means by which she indulged it, so she more than equalled her in the ingratitude of an unnatural son and a parricide. She is said to have left behind her some memoirs, of which Tacitus availed himself in the composition of his Annals.

In this reign, the conquest of the Britons still continued to be the principal object of military enterprise, and Suetonius Paulinus was invested with the command of the Roman army employed in the reduction of that people. The island of Mona, now Anglesey, being the chief seat of the Druids, he resolved to commence his operations with attacking a place which was the centre of superstition, and to which the vanquished Britons retreated as the last asylum of liberty. The inhabitants endeavoured, both by force of arms and the terrors of religion, to obstruct his landing on this sacred island. The women and Druids assembled promiscuously with the soldiers upon the shore, where running about in wild disorder, with flaming torches in their hands, and pouring forth the most hideous exclamations, they struck the Romans with consternation. But Suetonius animating his troops, they boldly attacked the inhabitants, routed them in the field, and burned the Druids in the same fires which had been prepared by those priests for the catastrophe of the invaders, destroying at the same time all the consecrated groves and altars in the island. Suetonius having thus triumphed over the religion of the Britons, flattered himself with the hopes of soon effecting the reduction of the people. But they, encouraged by his absence, had taken arms, and under the conduct of Boadicea, queen of the Iceni, who had been treated in the most ignominious manner by the Roman tribunes, had already driven the hateful invaders from their several settlements. Suetonius hastened to the protection of London, which was by this time a flourishing Roman colony; but he found upon his arrival, that any attempt to preserve it would be attended with the utmost danger to the army. London therefore was reduced to ashes; and the Romans, and all strangers, to the number of seventy thousand, were put to the sword without distinction, the Britons seeming determined to convince the enemy that they would acquiesce in no other terms than a total evacuation of the island. This massacre, however, was revenged by Suetonius in a decisive engagement, where eighty thousand of the Britons are said to have been killed; after which, Boadicea, to avoid falling into the hands of the insolent conquerors, put a period to her own life by means of poison. It being judged unadvisable that Suetonius should any longer conduct the war against a people whom he had exasperated by his severity, he was recalled, and Petronius Turpilianus appointed in his room. The command was afterwards given successively to Trebellius Maximus and Vettius Bolanus; but the plan pursued by these generals was only to retain, by a conciliatory administration, the parts of the island which had already submitted to the Roman arms.

During these transactions in Britain, Nero himself was exhibiting, in Rome or some of the provinces, such scenes of extravagance as almost exceed credibility. In one place, entering the lists amongst the competitors in a chariot race; in another, contending for victory with the common musicians on the stage; revelling in open day in the company of the most abandoned prostitutes and the vilest of men; in the night, committing depredations on the peaceful inhabitants of the capital; polluting with detestable lust, or drenching with human blood, the streets, the palace, and the habitations of private families; and, to crown his enormities, setting fire to Rome, while he sung with delight in beholding the dreadful conflagration. In vain would history be ransacked for a parallel to this emperor, who united the most shameful vices to the most extravagant vanity, the most abject meanness to the strongest but most preposterous ambition; and the whole of whose life was one continued scene of lewdness, sensuality, rapine, cruelty, and folly. It is emphatically observed by Tacitus, "that Nero, after the murder of many illustrious personages, manifested a desire of extirpating virtue itself."

Among the excesses of Nero's reign, are to be mentioned the horrible cruelties exercised against the Christians in various parts of the empire, in which inhuman transactions the natural barbarity of the emperor was inflamed by the prejudices and interested policy of the pagan priesthood.

The tyrant scrupled not to charge them with the act of burning Rome; and he satiated his fury against them by such outrages as are unexampled in history. They were covered with the skins of wild beasts, and torn by dogs; were crucified, and set on fire, that they might serve for lights in the night-time. Nero offered his gardens for this spectacle, and exhibited the games of the Circus by this dreadful illumination. Sometimes they were covered with wax and other combustible materials, after which a sharp stake was put under their chin, to make them stand upright, and they were burnt alive, to give light to the spectators.

In the person of Nero, it is observed by Suetonius, the race of the Caesars became extinct; a race rendered illustrious by the first and second emperors, but which their successors no less disgraced. The despotism of Julius Caesar, though haughty and imperious, was liberal and humane: that of Augustus, if we exclude a few instances of vindictive severity towards individuals, was mild and conciliating; but the reigns of Tiberius, Caligula, and Nero (for we except Claudius from part of the censure), while discriminated from each other by some peculiar circumstances, exhibited the most flagrant acts of licentiousness and perverted authority. The most abominable lust, the most extravagant luxury, the most shameful rapaciousness, and the most inhuman cruelty, constitute the general characteristics of those capricious and detestable tyrants. Repeated experience now clearly refuted the opinion of Augustus, that he had introduced amongst the Romans the best form of government: but while we make this observation, it is proper to remark, that, had he even restored the republic, there is reason to believe that the nation would again have been soon distracted with internal divisions, and a perpetual succession of civil wars. The manners of the people were become too dissolute to be restrained by the authority of elective and temporary magistrates; and the Romans were hastening to that fatal period when general and great corruption, with its attendant debility, would render them an easy prey to any foreign invaders.

But the odious government of the emperors was not the only grievance under which the people laboured in those disastrous times: patrician avarice concurred with imperial rapacity to increase the sufferings of the nation. The senators, even during the commonwealth, had become openly corrupt in the dispensation of public justice; and under the government of the emperors pernicious abuse was practised to a yet greater extent. That class being now, equally with other Roman citizens, dependent on the sovereign power, their sentiments of duty and honour were degraded by the loss of their former dignity; and being likewise deprived of the lucrative governments of provinces, to which they had annually succeeded by an elective rotation in the times of the republic, they endeavoured to compensate the reduction of their emoluments by an unbounded venality in the judicial decisions of the forum. Every source of national happiness and prosperity was by this means destroyed. The possession of property became precarious; industry, in all its branches, was effectually discouraged, and the amor patriae, which had formerly been the animating principle of the nation, was almost universally extinguished.

It is a circumstance corresponding to the general singularity of the present reign, that, of the few writers who flourished in it, and whose works have been transmitted to posterity, two ended their days by the order of the emperor, and the third, from indignation at his conduct. These unfortunate victims were Seneca, Petronius Arbiter, and Lucan.

SENECA was born about six years before the Christian aera, and gave early indication of uncommon talents. His father, who had come from Corduba to Rome, was a man of letters, particularly fond of declamation, in which he instructed his son, and placed him, for the acquisition of philosophy, under the most celebrated stoics of that age. Young Seneca, imbibing the precepts of the Pythagorean doctrine, religiously abstained from eating the flesh of animals, until Tiberius having threatened to punish some Jews and Egyptians, who abstained from certain meats, he was persuaded by his father to renounce the Pythagorean practice. Seneca displayed the talents of an eloquent speaker; but dreading the jealousy of Caligula, who aspired to the same excellence, he thought proper to abandon that pursuit, and apply himself towards suing for the honours and offices of the state. He accordingly obtained the place of quaestor, in which office incurring the imputation of a scandalous amour with Julia Livia, he removed from Rome, and was banished by the emperor Claudius to Corsica.

Upon the marriage of Claudius with Agrippina, Seneca was recalled from his exile, in which he had remained near eight years, and was appointed to superintend the education of Nero, now destined to become the successor to the throne. In the character of preceptor he appears to have acquitted himself with ability and credit; though he has been charged by his enemies with having initiated his pupil in those detestable vices which disgraced the reign of Nero. Could he have indeed been guilty of such immoral conduct, it is probable that he would not so easily have forfeited the favour of that emperor; and it is more reasonable to suppose, that his disapprobation of Nero's conduct was the real cause of that odium which soon after proved fatal to him. By the enemies whom distinguished merit and virtue never fail to excite at a profligate court, Seneca was accused of having maintained a criminal correspondence with Agrippina in the life-time of Claudius; but the chief author of this calumny was Suilius, who had been banished from Rome at the instance of Seneca. He was likewise charged with having amassed exorbitant riches, with having built magnificent houses, and formed beautiful gardens, during the four years in which he had acted as preceptor to Nero. This charge he considered as a prelude to his destruction; which to avoid, if possible, he requested of the emperor to accept of the riches and possessions which he had acquired in his situation at court, and to permit him to withdraw himself into a life of studious retirement. Nero, dissembling his secret intentions, refused this request; and Seneca, that he might obviate all cause of suspicion or offence, kept himself at home for some time, under the pretext of indisposition.

Upon the breaking out of the conspiracy of Piso, in which some of the principal senators were concerned, Natalis, the discoverer of the plot, mentioned Seneca's name, as an accessory. There is, however, no satisfactory evidence that Seneca had any knowledge of the plot. Piso, according to the declaration of Natalis, had complained that he never saw Seneca; and the latter had observed, in answer, that it was not conducive to their common interest to see each other often. Seneca likewise pleaded indisposition, and said that his own life depended upon the safety of Piso's person. Nero, however, glad of such an occasion of sacrificing the philosopher to his secret jealousy, sent him an order to destroy himself. When the messenger arrived with this mandate, Seneca was sitting at table, with his wife Paulina and two of his friends. He heard the message not only with philosophical firmness, but even with symptoms of joy, and observed, that such an honour might long have been expected from a man who had assassinated all his friends, and even murdered his own mother. The only request which he made, was, that he might be permitted to dispose of his possessions as he pleased; but this was refused him. Immediately turning himself to his friends, who were weeping at his melancholy fate, he said to them, that, since he could not leave them what he considered as his own property, he should leave at least his own life for an example; an innocence of conduct which they might imitate, and by which they might acquire immortal fame. He remonstrated with composure against their unavailing tears and lamentations, and asked them, whether they had not learnt better to sustain the shocks of fortune, and the violence of tyranny?

The emotions of his wife he endeavoured to allay with philosophical consolation; and when she expressed a resolution to die with him, he said, that he was glad to find his example imitated with so much fortitude. The veins of both were opened at the same time; but Nero's command extending only to Seneca, the life of Paulina was preserved; and, according to some authors, she was not displeased at being prevented from carrying her precipitate resolution into effect. Seneca's veins bleeding but slowly, an opportunity was offered him of displaying in his last moments a philosophical magnanimity similar to that of Socrates; and it appears that his conversation during this solemn period was maintained with dignified composure. To accelerate his lingering fate, he drank a dose of poison; but this producing no effect, he ordered his attendants to carry him into a warm bath, for the purpose of rendering the haemorrhage from his veins more copious. This expedient proving likewise ineffectual, and the soldiers who witnessed the execution of the emperor's order being clamorous for its accomplishment, he was removed into a stove, and suffocated by the steam. He underwent his fate on the 12th of April, in the sixty-fifth year of the Christian aera, and the fifty-third year of his age. His body was burnt, and his ashes deposited in a private manner, according to his will, which had been made during the period when he was in the highest degree of favour with Nero.

The writings of Seneca are numerous, and on various subjects. His first composition, addressed to Novacus, is on Anger, and continued through three books. After giving a lively description of this passion, the author discusses a variety of questions concerning it: he argues strongly against its utility, in contradiction to the peripatetics, and recommends its restraint, by many just and excellent considerations. This treatise may be regarded, in its general outlines, as a philosophical amplification of the passage in Horace:—

> Ira furor brevis est: animum rege; qui, nisi paret,
> Imperat: hunc fraenis, hunc tu compesce catena.
> Epist. I. ii.

> Anger's a fitful madness: rein thy mind,
> Subdue the tyrant, and in fetters bind,
> Or be thyself the slave.

The next treatise is on Consolation, addressed to his mother, Helvia, and was written during his exile. He there informs his mother that he bears his banishment with fortitude, and advises her to do the same. He observes, that, in respect to himself, change of place, poverty, ignominy, and contempt, are not real evils; that there may be two reasons for her anxiety on his account; first, that, by his absence, she is deprived of his protection; and in the next place, of the satisfaction arising from his company; on both which heads he suggests a variety of pertinent observations. Prefixed to this treatise, are some epigrams written on the banishment of Seneca, but whether or not by himself, is uncertain.

Immediately subsequent to the preceding, is another treatise on Consolation, addressed to one of Claudius's freedmen, named Polybius, perhaps after the learned historian. In this tract, which is in several parts mutilated, the author endeavours to console Polybius for the loss of a brother who had lately died. The sentiments and admonitions are well suggested for the purpose; but they are intermixed with such fulsome encomiums on the imperial domestic, as degrade the dignity of the author, and can be ascribed to no other motive than that of endeavouring to procure a recall from his exile, through the interest of Polybius.

A fourth treatise on Consolation is addressed to Marcia, a respectable and opulent lady, the daughter of Cremutius Cordus, by whose death she was deeply affected. The author, besides many consolatory arguments, proposes for her imitation a number of examples, by attending to which she may be enabled to overcome a passion that is founded only in too great sensibility of mind. The subject is ingeniously prosecuted, not without the occasional mixture of some delicate flattery, suitable to the character of the correspondent.

These consolatory addresses are followed by a treatise on Providence, which evinces the author to have entertained the most just and philosophical sentiments on that subject. He infers the necessary existence of a Providence from the regularity and constancy observed in the government of the universe but his chief object is to show, why, upon the principle that a Providence exists, good men should be liable to evils. The enquiry is conducted with a variety of just observations, and great force of argument; by which the author vindicates the goodness and wisdom of the Almighty, in a strain of sentiment corresponding to the most approved suggestions of natural religion.

The next treatise, which is on Tranquillity of Mind, appears to have been written soon after his return from exile. There is a confusion in the arrangement of this tract; but it contains a variety of just observations, and may be regarded as a valuable production.

Then follows a discourse on the Constancy of a Wise Man. This has by some been considered as a part of the preceding treatise; but they are evidently distinct. It is one of the author's best productions, in regard both of sentiment and composition, and contains a fund of moral observations, suited to fortify the mind under the oppression of accidental calamities.

We next meet with a tract on Clemency, in two books, addressed to Nero. This appears to have been written in the beginning of the reign of Nero, on whom the author bestows some high encomiums, which, at that time, seem not to have been destitute of foundation. The discourse abounds with just observation, applicable to all ranks of men; and, if properly attended to by that infatuated emperor, might have prevented the perpetration of those acts of cruelty, which, with his other extravagancies, have rendered his name odious to posterity.

The discourse which succeeds is on the Shortness of Life, addressed to Paulinus. In this excellent treatise the author endeavours to show, that the complaint of the shortness of life is not founded in truth: that it is men who make life short, either by passing it in indolence, or otherwise improperly. He inveighs against indolence, luxury, and every unprofitable avocation; observing, that the best use of time is to apply it to the study of wisdom, by which life may be rendered sufficiently long.

Next follows a discourse on a Happy Life, addressed to Gallio. Seneca seems to have intended this as a vindication of himself, against those who calumniated him on account of his riches and manner of living. He maintained that a life can only be rendered happy by its conformity to the dictates of virtue, but that such a life is perfectly compatible with the possession of riches, where they happen to accrue. The author pleads his own cause with great ability, as well as justness of argument. His vindication is in many parts highly beautiful, and accompanied with admirable sentiments respecting the moral obligations to a virtuous life. The conclusion of this discourse bears no similarity, in point of composition, to the preceding parts, and is evidently spurious.

The preceding discourse is followed by one upon the Retirement of a Wise Man. The beginning of this tract is wanting; but in the sequel the author discusses a question which was much agitated amongst the Stoics and Epicureans, viz., whether a wise man ought to concern himself with the affairs of the public. Both these sects of philosophers maintained that a life of retirement was most suitable to a wise man, but they differed with respect to the circumstances in which it might be proper to deviate from this conduct;

one party considering the deviation as prudent, when there existed a just motive for such conduct, and the other, when there was no forcible reason against it. Seneca regards both these opinions as founded upon principles inadequate to the advancement both of public and private happiness, which ought ever to be the ultimate object of moral speculation.

The last of the author's discourses, addressed to Aebucius, is on Benefits, and continued through seven books. He begins with lamenting the frequency of ingratitude amongst mankind, a vice which he severely censures. After some preliminary considerations respecting the nature of benefits, he proceeds to show in what manner, and on whom, they ought to be conferred. The greater part of these books is employed on the solution of abstract questions relative to benefits, in the manner of Chrysippus; where the author states explicitly the arguments on both sides, and from the full consideration of them, deduces rational conclusions.

The Epistles of Seneca consist of one hundred and twenty-four, all on moral subjects. His Natural Questions extend through seven books, in which he has collected the hypotheses of Aristotle and other ancient writers. These are followed by a whimsical effusion on the death of Caligula. The remainder of his works comprises seven Persuasive Discourses, five books of Controversies, and ten books containing Extracts of Declamations.

From the multiplicity of Seneca's productions, it is evident, that, notwithstanding the luxurious life he is said to have led, he was greatly devoted to literature, a propensity which, it is probable, was confirmed by his banishment during almost eight years in the island of Corsica, where he was in a great degree secluded from every other resource of amusement to a cultivated mind. But with whatever splendour Seneca's domestic economy may have been supported, it seems highly improbable that he indulged himself in luxurious enjoyment to any vicious excess. His situation at the Roman court, being honourable and important, could not fail of being likewise advantageous, not only from the imperial profusion common at that time, but from many contingent emoluments which his extensive interest and patronage would naturally afford him. He was born of a respectable rank, lived in habits of familiar intercourse with persons of the first distinction, and if, in the course of his attendance upon Nero, he had acquired a large fortune, no blame could justly attach to his conduct in maintaining an elegant hospitality. The imputation of luxury was thrown upon him from two quarters, viz, by the dissolute companions of Nero, to whom the mention of such an example served as an apology for their own extreme dissipation; and by those who envied him for the affluence and dignity which he had acquired. The charge, however, is supported only by vague assertion, and is discredited by every consideration which ought to have weight in determining the reality of human characters. It seems totally inconsistent with his habits of literary industry, with the virtuous sentiments which he every where strenuously maintains, and the esteem with which he was regarded by a numerous acquaintance, as a philosopher and a moralist.

The writings of Seneca have been traduced almost equally with his manner of living, though in both he has a claim to indulgence, from the fashion of the times. He is more studious of minute embellishments in style than the writers of the Augustan age; and the didactic strain, in which he mostly prosecutes his subjects, has a tendency to render him sententious; but the expression of his thoughts is neither enfeebled by decoration, nor involved in obscurity by conciseness. He is not more rich in artificial ornament than in moral admonition. Seneca has been charged with depreciating former writers, to render himself more conspicuous; a charge which, so far as appears from his writings, is founded rather in negative than positive testimony. He has not endeavoured to establish his fame by any affectation of singularity in doctrine; and while he passes over in silence the names of illustrious authors, he avails himself with judgment of the most valuable stores with which they had enriched philosophy. On the whole, he is an author whose principles may be adopted not only with safety, but great advantage; and his writings merit a degree of consideration, superior to what they have hitherto ever enjoyed in the literary world.

Seneca, besides his prose works, was the author of some tragedies. The Medea, the Troas, and the Hippolytus, are ascribed to him. His father is said to have written the Hercules Furens, Thyestes, Agamemnon, and Hercules Oetaeus. The three remaining tragedies, the Thebais, Oedipus, and Octavia, usually published in the same collection with the seven preceding, are supposed to be the productions of other authors, but of whom, is uncertain. These several pieces are written in a neat style; the plots and characters are conducted with an attention to probability and nature: but none of them is so forcible, in point of tragical distress, as to excite in the reader any great degree of emotion.—

PETRONIUS was a Roman knight, and apparently of considerable fortune. In his youth he seems to have given great application to polite literature, in which he acquired a justness of taste, as well as an elegance of composition. Early initiated in the gaieties of fashionable life, he contracted a habit of voluptuousness which rendered him an accommodating companion to the dissipated and the luxurious. The court of Claudius, entirely governed for some time by Messalina, was then the residence of pleasure; and here Petronius failed not of making a conspicuous appearance. More delicate, however, than sensual, he rather joined in the dissipation, than indulged in the vices of the palace. To interrupt a course of life too uniform to afford him perpetual satisfaction, he accepted of the proconsulship of Bithynia, and went to that province, where he discharged the duties of his office with great credit. Upon his return to Rome, Nero, who had succeeded Claudius, made him consul, in recompense of his services. This new dignity, by giving him frequent and easy access to the emperor, created an intimacy between them, which was increased to friendship and esteem on the side of Nero, by the elegant entertainments often given him by Petronius. In a short time, this gay voluptuary became so much a favourite at court, that nothing was agreeable but what was approved by Petronius and the authority which he acquired, by being umpire in whatever related to the economy of gay dissipation, procured him the title of Arbiter elegantiarum. Things continued in this state whilst the emperor kept within the bounds of moderation; and Petronius acted as intendant of his pleasures, ordering him shows, games, comedies, music, feats, and all that could contribute to make the hours of relaxation pass agreeably; seasoning, at the same time, the innocent delights which he procured for the emperor with every possible charm, to prevent him from seeking after such as might prove pernicious both to morals and the republic. Nero, however, giving way to his own disposition, which was naturally vicious, at length changed his conduct, not only in regard to the government of the empire, but of himself and listening to other counsels than those of Petronius, gave the entire reins to his passions, which afterwards plunged him in ruin. The emperor's new favourite was Tigellinus, a man of the most profligate morals, who omitted nothing that could gratify the inordinate appetites of his prince, at the expense of all decency and virtue. During this period, Petronius gave vent to his indignation, in the satire transmitted under his name by the title of Satyricon. But his total retirement from court did not secure him from the artifices of Tigellinus, who laboured with all his power to destroy the man whom he had industriously supplanted in the emperor's favour. With this view he insinuated to Nero, that Petronius was too intimately connected with Scevinus not to be engaged in Piso's conspiracy; and, to support his calumny, caused the emperor to be present at the examination of one of Petronius's slaves, whom he had secretly suborned to swear against his master. After this

The Lives of the Twelve Caesars - Nero

transaction, to deprive Petronius of all means of justifying himself, they threw into prison the greatest part of his domestics. Nero embraced with joy the opportunity of removing a man, to whom he knew the present manners of the court were utterly obnoxious, and he soon after issued orders for arresting Petronius. As it required, however, some time to deliberate whether they should put a person of his consideration to death, without more evident proofs of the charges preferred against him, such was his disgust at living in the power of so detestable and capricious a tyrant, that he resolved to die. For this purpose, making choice of the same expedient which had been adopted by Seneca, he caused his veins to be opened, but he closed them again, for a little time, that he might enjoy the conversation of his friends, who came to see him in his last moments. He desired them, it is said, to entertain him, not with discourses on the immortality of the soul, or the consolation of philosophy, but with agreeable tales and poetic gallantries. Disdaining to imitate the servility of those who, dying by the orders of Nero, yet made him their heir, and filled their wills with encomiums on the tyrant and his favourites, he broke to pieces a goblet of precious stones, out of which he had commonly drank, that Nero, who he knew would seize upon it after his death, might not have the pleasure of using it. As the only present suitable to such a prince, he sent him, under a sealed cover, his Satyricon, written purposely against him; and then broke his signet, that it might not, after his death, become the means of accusation against the person in whose custody it should be found.

The Satyricon of Petronius is one of the most curious productions in the Latin language. Novel in its nature, and without any parallel in the works of antiquity, some have imagined it to be a spurious composition, fabricated about the time of the revival of learning in Europe. This conjecture, however, is not more destitute of support, than repugnant to the most circumstantial evidence in favour of its authenticity. Others, admitting the work to be a production of the age of Nero, have questioned the design with which it was written, and have consequently imputed to the author a most immoral intention. Some of the scenes, incidents, and characters, are of so extraordinary a nature, that the description of them, without a particular application, must have been regarded as extremely whimsical, and the work, notwithstanding its ingenuity, has been doomed to perpetual oblivion: but history justifies the belief, that in the court of Nero, the extravagancies mentioned by Petronius were realized to a degree which authenticates the representation given of them. The inimitable character of Trimalchio, which exhibits a person sunk in the most debauched effeminacy, was drawn for Nero; and we are assured, that there were formerly medals of that emperor, with these words, C. Nero August. Imp., and on the reverse, Trimalchio. The various characters are well discriminated, and supported with admirable propriety. Never was such licentiousness of description united to such delicacy of colouring. The force of the satire consists not in poignancy of sentiment, but in the ridicule which arises from the whimsical, but characteristic and faithful exhibition of the objects introduced. That Nero was struck with the justness of the representation, is evident from the displeasure which he showed, at finding Petronius so well acquainted with his infamous excesses. After levelling his suspicion on all who could possibly have betrayed him, he at last fixed on a senator's wife, named Silia, who bore a part in his revels, and was an intimate friend of Petronius upon which she was immediately sent into banishment. Amongst the miscellaneous materials in this work, are some pieces of poetry, written in an elegant taste. A poem on the civil war between Caesar and Pompey, is beautiful and animated.

Though the Muses appear to have been mostly in a quiescent state from the time of Augustus, we find from Petronius Arbiter, who exhibits the manners of the capital during the reign of Nero, that poetry still continued to be a favourite pursuit amongst the Romans, and one to which, indeed, they seem to have had a national propensity.

   ——Ecce inter pocula quaerunt
Romulidae saturi, quid dia poemata narrent.—Persius, Sat. i. 30.

   —Nay, more! Our nobles, gorged, and swilled with wine,
Call o'er the banquet for a lay divine!—Gifford.

It was cultivated as a kind of fashionable exercise, in short and desultory attempts, in which the chief ambition was to produce verses extempore. They were publicly recited by their authors with great ostentation; and a favourable verdict from an audience, however partial, and frequently obtained either by intrigue or bribery, was construed by those frivolous pretenders into a real adjudication of poetical fame.

The custom of publicly reciting poetical compositions, with the view of obtaining the opinion of the hearers concerning them, and for which purpose Augustus had built the Temple of Apollo, was well calculated for the improvement of taste and judgment, as well as the excitement of emulation;

but, conducted as it now was, it led to a general degradation of poetry. Barbarism in language, and a corruption of taste, were the natural consequences of this practice, while the judgment of the multitude was either blind or venal, and while public approbation sanctioned the crudities of hasty composition. There arose, however, in this period, some candidates for the bays, who carried their efforts beyond the narrow limits which custom and inadequate genius prescribed to the poetical exertions of their contemporaries. Amongst these were Lucan and Persius.—

LUCAN was the son of Annaeus Mela, the brother of Seneca, the philosopher. He was born at Corduba, the original residence of the family, but came early to Rome, where his promising talents, and the patronage of his uncle, recommended him to the favour of Nero; by whom he was raised to the dignity of an augur and quaestor before he had attained the usual age. Prompted by the desire of displaying his political abilities, he had the imprudence to engage in a competition with his imperial patron. The subject chosen by Nero was the tragical fate of Niobe; and that of Lucan was Orpheus. The ease with which the latter obtained the victory in the contest, excited the jealousy of the emperor, who resolved upon depressing his rising genius. With this view, he exposed him daily to the mortification of fresh insults, until at last the poet's resentment was so much provoked, that he entered into the conspiracy of Piso for cutting off the tyrant. The plot being discovered, there remained for the unfortunate Lucan no hope of pardon: and choosing the same mode of death which was employed by his uncle, he had his veins opened, while he sat in a warm bath, and expired in pronouncing with great emphasis the following lines in his Pharsalia:—

   Scinditur avulsus; nec sicut vulnere sanguis
   Emicuit lentus: ruptis cadit undique venis;
   Discursusque animae diversa in membra meantis
   Interceptus aquis, nullius, vita perempti
   Est tanta dimissa via.—Lib. iii. 638.

             —Asunder flies the man.
   No single wound the gaping rupture seems,
   Where trickling crimson flows in tender streams;
   But from an opening horrible and wide
   A thousand vessels pour the bursting tide;
   At once the winding channel's course was broke,

Where wandering life her mazy journey took.—Rowe.

Some authors have said that he betrayed pusillanimity at the hour of death; and that, to save himself from punishment, he accused his mother of being involved in the conspiracy. This circumstance, however, is not mentioned by other writers, who relate, on the contrary, that he died with philosophical fortitude. He was then only in the twenty-sixth year of his age.

Lucan had scarcely reached the age of puberty when he wrote a poem on the contest between Hector and Achilles. He also composed in his youth a poem on the burning of Rome; but his only surviving work is the Pharsalia, written on the civil war between Caesar and Pompey. This poem, consisting of ten books, is unfinished, and its character has been more depreciated than that of any other production of antiquity. In the plan of the poem, the author prosecutes the different events in the civil war, beginning his narrative at the passage of the Rubicon by Caesar. He invokes not the muses, nor engages any gods in the dispute; but endeavours to support an epic dignity by vigour of sentiment, and splendour of description. The horrors of civil war, and the importance of a contest which was to determine the fate of Rome and the empire of the world, are displayed with variety of colouring, and great energy of expression. In the description of scenes, and the recital of heroic actions, the author discovers a strong and lively imagination; while, in those parts of the work which are addressed either to the understanding or the passions, he is bold, figurative, and animated. Indulging too much in amplification, he is apt to tire with prolixity; but in all his excursions he is ardent, elevated, impressive, and often brilliant. His versification has not the smoothness which we admire in the compositions of Virgil, and his language is often involved in the intricacies of technical construction: but with all his defects, his beauties are numerous; and he discovers a greater degree of merit than is commonly found in the productions of a poet of twenty-six years of age, at which time he died.——

PERSIUS was born at Volaterrae, of an equestrian family, about the beginning of the Christian aera. His father dying when he was six years old, he was left to the care of his mother, for whom and for his sisters he expresses the warmest affection. At the age of twelve he came to Rome, where, after attending a course of grammar and rhetoric under the respective masters of those branches of education, he placed himself under the tuition of Annaeus Cornutus, a celebrated stoic philosopher of that time. There subsisted between him and this preceptor so great a friendship, that at his death, which happened in the twenty-ninth year of his age, he bequeathed to Cornutus a handsome sum of money, and his library. The latter, however, accepting only the books, left the money to Persius's sisters.

Priscian, Quintilian, and other ancient writers, spear of Persius's satires as consisting of a book without any division. They have since, however, been generally divided into six different satires, but by some only into five. The subjects of these compositions are, the vanity of the poets in his time; the backwardness of youth to the cultivation of moral science; ignorance and temerity in political administration, chiefly in allusion to the government of Nero: the fifth satire is employed in evincing that the wise man also is free; in discussing which point, the author adopts the observations used by Horace on the same subject. The last satire of Persius is directed against avarice. In the fifth, we meet with a beautiful address to Cornutus, whom the author celebrates for his amiable virtues, and peculiar talents for teaching. The following lines, at the same time that they show how diligently the preceptor and his pupil were employed through the whole day in the cultivation of moral science, afford a more agreeable picture of domestic comfort and philosophical conviviality, than might be expected in the family of a rigid stoic:

>   Tecum etenim longos memini consumere soles,
>   Et tecum primas epulis decerpere noctes.
>   Unum opus, et requiem pariter disponimus ambo:
>   Atque verecunda laxamus feria mensa.—Sat. v.

>   Can I forget how many a summer's day,
>   Spent in your converse, stole, unmarked, away?
>   Or how, while listening with increased delight,
>   I snatched from feasts the earlier hours of night?—Gifford.

The satires of Persius are written in a free, expostulatory, and argumentative manner; possessing the same justness of sentiment as those of Horace, but exerted in the way of derision, and not with the admirable raillery of that facetious author. They are regarded by many as obscure; but this imputation arises more from unacquaintance with the characters and manners to which the author alludes, than from any peculiarity either in his language or composition. His versification is harmonious; and we have only to remark, in addition to similar examples in other Latin writers, that, though Persius is acknowledged to have been both virtuous and modest, there are in the fourth satire a few passages which cannot decently admit of being translated. Such was the freedom of the Romans, in the use of some expressions, which just refinement has now exploded.—

Another poet, in this period, was FABRICIUS VEIENTO, who wrote a severe satire against the priests of his time; as also one against the senators, for corruption in their judicial capacity. Nothing remains of either of those productions; but, for the latter, the author was banished by Nero.

There now likewise flourished a lyric poet, CAESIUS BASSUS, to whom Persius has addressed his sixth satire. He is said to have been, next to Horace, the best lyric poet among the Romans; but of his various compositions, only a few inconsiderable fragments are preserved.

To the two poets now mentioned must be added POMPONIUS SECUNDUS, a man of distinguished rank in the army, and who obtained the honour of a triumph for a victory over a tribe of barbarians in Germany. He wrote several tragedies, which in the judgment of Quintilian, were beautiful compositions.